Critters
of Michigan

ALEX TROUTMAN

produced in cooperation with Wildlife Forever

About Wildlife Forever

Wildlife Forever works to conserve America's outdoor heritage through conservation education, preservation of habitat, and scientific management of fish and wildlife. Wildlife Forever is a 501c3 nonprofit organization dedicated to restoring habitat and teaching the next generation about conservation.

Become a member and learn more about innovative programs like the Art of Conservation®, Fish and Songbird Art Contests®, Clean Drain Dry Initiative™, and Prairie City USA®. For more information, visit wildlifeforever.org.

Front cover photos by **Bryant Aardema/shutterstock.com:** Long-tailed Weasel, **Paul Reeves Photography/shutterstock.com:** Northern Leopard Frog, **Rabbitti/shutterstock.com:** Eastern Cottontail
Back cover photo by **Mike Truchon/Shutterstock.com:** Blue Jay

Edited by Brett Ortler and Jenna Barron
Cover and book design by Jonathan Norberg
Proofreader: Emily Beaumont

10 9 8 7 6 5 4 3 2 1

Critters of Michigan
First Edition 2000, Second Edition 2023
Copyright © 2000 by Wildlife Forever, Copyright © 2023 by Alex Troutman
The first edition (2000) of this book was produced by Wildlife Forever.
AdventureKEEN is grateful for its continued partnership and advocacy on behalf of the natural world.

Published by Adventure Publications
An imprint of AdventureKEEN
310 Garfield Street South, Cambridge, Minnesota 55008
(800) 678-7006
www.adventurepublications.net
All rights reserved
Printed in China
Cataloging-in-Publication data is available from the Library of Congress
ISBN 978-1-64755-351-7 (pbk.); 978-1-64755-352-4 (ebook)

Acknowledgments

I want to thank everyone who believed in and supported me over the years—a host of friends, family, and teachers. I want to especially thank my mom and my siblings Van, Bre, and TJ.

Dedication

I dedicate this book to my brother Van:
May you continue to enjoy the birds and wildlife in heaven.

Next, this book is for all the kids who have a passion for nature and the outdoors, especially ones who identify as Black, Brown, Indigenous, and People of Color. May this be an encouragement to never give up, and if you have a dream and passion for something, pursue it relentlessly. I also hope to set an example that you can be your full, authentic self and be successful without having to hide who you are!

Lastly, I dedicate this book to all those with ADHD, dyslexia, and all other members of the Neurodivergent community. While our quirks make things more challenging, our goals are not impossible to reach; sometimes it takes a little more time and help, but we, too, can succeed!

Contents

4

Reptiles and Amphibians

Introduction

My passion for nature started when I was young. I was always amazed by the sunlit fiery glow of the Red-tailed Hawks as they soared overhead when I went fishing with my family. The Red-tailed Hawk was my spark bird—the bird that captures your attention and gets you into birding. Through my many encounters with Red-tailed Hawks, and other species like Garter Snakes and coyotes, I found a passion for nature and the environment. Stumbling across conservationists like Steve Irwin, Jeff Corwin, and Jack Hanna introduced me to the field of Wildlife Biology as a career and gave birth to a dream that I was able to accomplish and live out: serving as a Fish and Wildlife Biologist for governmental agencies, as well as in the private sector.

My childhood dream was driven by a desire to learn more about the different types of ecosystems and the animals that call our wild places home. Books and field guides like this one whet my thirst for knowledge. Even before I could fully understand the words on the pages, I was drawn to books and flashcards that had animals on them. I could identify every animal I was shown and tell a fact about it. I hope that this edition of *Critters of Michigan* can be the fuel that sustains your passion for not only learning about wildlife, but also for caring for the environment and making sure that all are welcome in the outdoors. For others, may this book be the spark that ignites a flame for wildlife preservation and environmental stewardship. I hope that this book inspires children from lower socioeconomic and minority backgrounds to pursue their dreams to the fullest and be unapologetically themselves.

By profession, I'm a Fish and Wildlife Biologist, and I'm a nature enthusiast through and through. My love for nature includes making sure that everyone has an equal opportunity to enjoy the outdoors in their own way. So, as you use this book, I encourage you to be intentional in inviting others to enjoy nature with you. Enjoy your discoveries and stay curious!

–Alex Troutman

Pure Michigan

Michigan is famous for its lakes, its weather (especially its cold winters), and its abundant wildlife. Michigan gets its name from the Ojibwe people, who have lived in Michigan for more than 1,000 years. In Ojibwe, the word *michi-gama* means "large lake." This name is a perfect fit for the state, which, despite being inland, has the second-largest amount of shoreline in the United States, losing only to Alaska. The Great Lakes (Lake Superior, Lake Erie, Lake Huron, and Lake Michigan) dominate the landscape, and Lake Michigan even divides the state's land in half. Together these lakes make up an astounding 20% of the world's fresh water.

Michigan has three biomes—large areas with different plant and animal communities. The southern part of the state is a mixture of savanna and prairie grasslands and deciduous forests. Grasslands, home to wildflowers, wild turkeys, and plenty of other wildlife, once made up a much larger part of the state but have declined due to farming and fire management programs. Deciduous trees (those that lose their leaves each year), such as maples, oaks, and aspens, are common throughout southeastern and central Michigan. Northern Michigan is predominantly made up of coniferous forests (trees that don't lose their leaves each year).

These many types of environments are home to a huge variety of animals and plants: the state is home to more than 60 different kinds of mammals, at least 450 bird species, and over 50 species of reptiles and amphibians, not to mention fish, countless insects and other creepy-crawlies, mushrooms, plants, and more.

The forests of Michigan may get much attention when it comes to animals, as they are host to elk, owls, and cougars, but amazing wildlife also exists in the massive lakes, rivers, and streams. This is your guide to the animals, birds, reptiles, and amphibians that call Michigan home.

Some of Michigan's most iconic plants, animals, and other natural resources are now officially recognized as state symbols. Get to know them below and see if you can spot them all! You'll probably encounter our state nickname and motto, so we've included them here too!

State Bird:
American Robin

State Reptile:
Painted Turtle

State Tree:
White Pine

State Flower:
Apple Blossom

State Fish:
Brook Trout

State Fossil:
Mastodon

State Stone:
Petoskey Stone

State Gemstone:
Chlorastrolite

State Nickname:
Wolverine State

State Motto:
If you seek
a pleasant
peninsula,
look about you.

How to Use This Guide

This book is your introduction to some of the wonderful critters found in Michigan; it includes 25 mammals, 29 birds, and 9 reptiles and amphibians. It includes some animals you probably already know, such as deer and American Robins, but others you may not know about, such as Hognose Snakes or Sandhill Cranes. We've selected the species in this book because they are widespread (Downy Woodpecker, page 92), abundant (White-tailed Deer, page 56), or well known (Moose, page 40) but rare.

The book is organized by type of animals: mammals, birds, and reptiles and amphibians. Within each section, the animals are in alphabetical order. If you'd like to look for a critter quickly, turn to the checklist (page 140), which you can also use to keep track of how many animals you've seen! For each species, you'll see a photo of the animal, along with neat facts and information on the animal's habitat, diet, its predators, how it raises its young, and more.

Safety Note

Nature can be unpredictable, so don't go outdoors alone, and always tell an adult if you're going outside. All wild animals should be treated with respect. If you see one—big or small—don't get close to it or attempt to touch or feed it. Instead, keep your distance and enjoy spotting it. If you can, snap some pictures with a camera or make a quick drawing using a sketchbook. If the animal is getting too close, is acting strangely, or seems sick or injured, tell an adult right away, as it might have rabies, a disease that can affect mammals. The good news is there's a rabies vaccine, so it's important to visit a doctor right away if you get bit or scratched by a wild animal.

Notes About Icons

Each species page includes basic information about each animal, from what it eats to how it survives the winter. The book also includes information that's neat to know; in the mammals section, each page includes a simple track illustration of each animal, with approximate track size included. And along the side, there is an example track pattern for each mammal, with the exception for those that primarily glide or fly (flying squirrels and bats).

On the left-hand page for each mammal, a rough-size illustration is included that shows how big each animal is compared to a basketball.

Also on the left-hand page, there are icons that tell you when each animal is most active: nocturnal (at night), diurnal (during the day), or crepuscular (at dawn/dusk), so you know when to look. If an animal has a "zzz" icon, it hibernates during the winter. Some animals hibernate every winter, and their internal processes (breathing and heartbeat) slow down almost entirely. Other animals only partially hibernate, but this still helps them save energy and survive through the coldest part of the year.

nocturnal
(active at night)

diurnal
(active during day)

crepuscular
(most active at
dawn and dusk)

hibernates/deep sleeper
(dormant during winter)

ground nest

cup nest

platform nest

cavity nest

migrates

On the left-hand side of each bird page, the nest for each species is shown along with information on whether or not the bird migrates; on the right-hand side, there's information on where it goes.

Did you know?

Badgers are solitary animals, but they will sometimes hunt with coyotes in a team. The coyote will chase prey into the badger's den, and the badger will chase or dig out the prey that coyotes like. The badger's den has one entrance with a pile of dirt next to it. When a badger is threatened, it will back into its burrow and show its teeth.

Size Comparison Most Active Track Size Hibernates

2¾"

American Badger

Taxidea taxus

Size: 2—3 feet long; weighs 8—25 pounds

Habitat: Savannas, grasslands, and meadows

Range: Can be found throughout Michigan and westward through the Great Plains to the West Coast

Food: Carnivores; they eat Pocket Gophers, moles, Ground Squirrels, and other rodents. They will also eat dead animals (or carrion), fish, reptiles, and a few types of birds, especially ground-nesting birds.

Den: Badgers are fossorial (a digging animal that spends a lot of time underground); they build many dens or burrows throughout their range. Most dens are used to store food, but badgers also use dens to sleep in and raise their young. Dens can be over 10 feet deep and 4 feet wide.

Young: Cubs are born, with eyes closed, usually in April or May in litters of 2—3. Extensive care is provided by the mom for up to 3 months. After another 2—3 months, the young will gain their independence.

Predators: Predators include bears, bobcats, cougars, coyotes, Gray Wolves, Golden Eagles, and humans.

Tracks: The front tracks are 2¾ inches long and 2 inches wide.

The American Badger is a short, bulky mammal with grayish to dirty-red fur. Badgers have a distinctive face with a series of cream-and-white stripes offset by a black face.

Did you know?

Beavers are rodents! Yes, these flat-tailed mammals are rodents, like rats and squirrels. In fact, they are the largest native rodents in North America. Just like other rodents, beavers have large incisors, which they use to chew through trees to build dams and dens. Beavers are the original wetland engineers. By damming rivers and streams, beavers create ponds and wetlands.

Size Comparison   Most Active   Track Size

6"

American Beaver

Castor canadensis

Size: Body is 25–30 inches long; tail is 9–13 inches long; weighs 30–70 pounds

Habitat: Wooded wetland areas near ponds, streams, and lakes

Range: Beavers can be found throughout Michigan and in much of the rest of the United States.

Food: Leaves, twigs, and stems; they also feed on fruits and aquatic plant roots; throughout the year they gather and store tree cuttings, which they eat in winter.

Den: A beaver's den is called a lodge. It consists of a pile of branches that is splattered with mud and vegetation. Lodges are constructed near or on the banks of lakes and streams and have exits and entrances that are underwater.

Young: Young beavers (kits) are born in late April through May and June in litters of 3–4. After two years they are considered mature and will be forced out of the den.

Predators: Bobcats, cougars, bears, wolves, and coyotes. Human trappers are major predators too.

Tracks: A beaver's front foot looks a lot like your hand; it has five fingers. The hind (back) foot is long, with five separate toes that have webbing or extra skin in between each pair.

Ranges from dark brown to reddish brown. They have a stocky body with hind legs that are longer than the front legs. Their body is covered in dense fur, but the tail is naked. A beaver's tail has special blood vessels that help it cool or warm its body.

Did you know?

Female bears weigh between 90 and 300 pounds and are smaller than the average adult human male in the US. But don't let their small size fool you; with a bite force around 800 pounds per square inch (PSI) and swiping force of over 400 pounds, these bears are not to be taken lightly.

Size Comparison   Most Active   Track Size   Hibernates

   7–9"

16

Black Bear

Ursus americanus

Size: 5–6 feet long (nose to tail); weighs 200–600 pounds; males are usually larger than females

Habitat: Forests, lowland areas, and swamps

Range: In Michigan, they can be found throughout the state. In the Upper Peninsula area of the state, the population is rapidly increasing.

Food: Berries, fish, seeded crops, small mammals, wild grapes, tree shoots, ants, bees, beavers, and even deer fawns

Den: Denning usually starts in December, with bears emerging in late March or April. Dens can be either dug (out of a hillside, for example) or constructed with materials such as leaves, grass, and moss.

Young: Two cubs are usually born at one time (a litter) from August to November. Cubs are born furless and blind, with pink skin. They are often born in January and weigh 8–16 ounces.

Predators: Humans and other bears. Sometimes, other carnivores, such as wolves, coyotes, or even bobcats, will prey on Black Bears. Cubs are especially vulnerable.

Tracks: Front print is usually 4–6 inches long and 3½–5 inches wide, with the hind foot being 6–7 inches long and 3½–5 inches wide. Both feet have five toes.

Black Bears are usually black in color, but they can be many different variations of black and brown. Some even have grayish, reddish, or blonde fur.

Did you know?

Bobcats get their name from their short tail! They have the largest range of all wild cats in the United States. Bobcats will climb trees to eat porcupines, and they can even hunt prey much larger than themselves; in fact, they can take down prey that is over four times their size, such as White-tailed Deer!

Size Comparison   Most Active   Track Size

Bobcat

Lynx rufus

Size: 27–48 inches head to tail; males weigh 30 pounds, while females weigh 24 pounds

Habitat: Dense forests, scrub areas (forests of low trees and bushes), swamps, and even some urban (city) areas

Range: In Michigan, they have been reported in every county of the state; they are widespread throughout the United States.

Food: Squirrels, birds, rabbits and Snowshoe Hares, and White-tailed Deer fawns; occasionally even adult deer and porcupines!

Den: Dense shrubs, caves, or even hollow trees; dens can be lined with leaves or with moss.

Young: Bobcats usually breed in early winter through spring. Females give birth to a litter of 2 to 4 kittens. Bobcats become independent around 7 to 8 months, and they reach reproductive maturity at 1 year for females and at 2 years for males.

Predators: Occasionally fishers and coyotes; humans also hunt and trap bobcats for fur.

Tracks: Roughly 2 inches wide; both front and back paws have four toe pads and a carpal pad (a pad below the toe pads).

Bobcats have a white stomach and a brown or pale-gray top with black spots. The tail usually has a black tip. They are crepuscular (say it, cre-pus-cue-lar), which means they are most active in the dawn and twilight hours.

Did you know?

Coyotes are the biggest group of large predators in Michigan. At one time, coyotes were only found in the central and western parts of the US, but now with the help of humans (eliminating predators and clearing forest), they can be found throughout most of the country.

Size Comparison   Most Active   Track Size

2"

Coyote
Canis latrans

Size: 3–4 feet long; weighs 21–50 pounds

Habitat: Urban and suburban areas, woodlands, grasslands, and farm fields

Range: Coyotes are found throughout Michigan. They are also found throughout the US and Mexico, the northern parts of Central America, and southern Canada.

Food: A variety of prey, including rodents, birds, deer, and often livestock

Den: Coyotes will dig their own dens but will often use old fox or badger dens, or hollow logs.

Young: 5–7 pups, independent around 8–10 months

Predators: Bears and wolves; humans trap and kill for pelts and to "protect" livestock.

Tracks: Four toes and a carpal pad (the single pad below the toe pads) can be seen on all four feet.

Coyotes have a brown, reddish-brown, or gray topcoat with a lighter gray to white belly. They have a longer muzzle than other wild canines. They are active mostly during the night (nocturnal) but also during the twilight and dawn hours (crepuscular).

Did you know?

Chipmunks get their name from the "chip" or alert calls they use when they sense a threat. Eastern Chipmunks are not fully herbivores (plant eaters); in fact, they eat a variety of things, including other mammals and amphibians, like frogs.

Size Comparison   Most Active   Track Size   Hibernates

¾"

z^z

Eastern Chipmunk

Tamias striatus

Size: Body is 3–6 inches long; tail is 3–4 inches long; weighs 2½–5½ ounces

Habitat: Suburban areas, woodlands, and dense scrub areas

Range: Found throughout Michigan, the eastern US, and southern Canada

Food: Berries, seeds, frogs, insects, and mice

Den: Has multiple chambers (or rooms); the entrance is usually hidden under brush, fallen trees, rock piles, and human-made landscaping items.

Young: 2–8 young (kits) per litter, 2 litters per year. Born blind and without fur. Weigh under an ounce at birth. Eyes open at 4 weeks, and it becomes independent at 8 weeks.

Predators: Coyotes, feral and outdoor house cats, snakes, weasels, bobcats, hawks, and owls

Tracks: The front foot has four digit (toe) pads and is ½ inch long; the hind foot has five digit pads and is just under ¾ of an inch.

Chipmunks are small rodents with brown base colors and seven alternating stripes. During winter, they will stay underground. They hide food in underground caches that they will feed on through the winter.

Did you know?
The Eastern Cottontail gets its name from its short, puffy tail that looks like a cotton ball. A cottontail can travel up to 18 miles per hour! Rabbits have great hearing and eyesight. They can almost see all the way around them (360 degrees). On days with high wind, they will bed down in a burrow because the wind interferes with their ability to hear and detect predators.

Size Comparison   Most Active   Track Size

3½"

Eastern Cottontail

Sylvilagus floridanus

Size: 16–19 inches long; weighs 1½–4 pounds

Habitat: Forests, swamps, orchards, deserts, and farm areas

Range: Found throughout Michigan; through the eastern US to Arizona and New Mexico; isolated ranges in the Pacific Northwest

Food: Clovers; grasses; wild strawberries; garden plants; and twigs of a variety of trees, including maple, oak, and sumac

Den: Rabbits don't dig dens; they bed in shallow, grassy, saucer-shaped depressions (holes) or under shrubs. They will sometimes use woodchuck dens in the winter.

Young: They usually have 2–4 kits at one time, but it's not uncommon to have 7 or more. Born naked and blind, they weigh about an ounce (about the same weight as a slice of bread) and gain weight very quickly.

Predators: Owls, weasels, humans, and foxes

Tracks: The front foot is an inch long with four toe pads; the hind foot is 3½ inches long.

An Eastern Cottontail sports thick brown fur with a white belly, a gray rump, and a white "cotton" tail. During the winter, it survives by eating bark off of fruit trees and shrubs.

Did you know?

The Eastern Fox Squirrel's bones appear pink under ultraviolet (UV) light, a type of light human eyes can't see. Squirrels accidentally help to plant trees by forgetting where they have buried nuts. Sometimes they pretend to bury nuts to throw off would-be nut thieves.

Size Comparison   Most Active   Track Size

2½"

Eastern Fox Squirrel

Sciurus niger

Size: 19–28 inches long; weighs 1–3 pounds

Habitat: Open woodlands, suburban areas, and dense forest

Range: They are found mostly in the Lower Peninsula of Michigan and throughout the eastern United States to Texas and as far north as the Dakotas.

Food: Acorns, seeds, nuts, insects such as moths and beetles, birds, eggs, and dead fish

Den: Ball-shaped dreys, or nests, are made of vegetation like leaves, sometimes in tree cavities.

Young: 2–3 kittens born between December and February or May and June. Kittens are born naked and weigh half an ounce; they are cared for by their parents for the first 7–8 weeks. They can reproduce by around 10–11 months for males and 8 months for females.

Predators: Humans, hawks, cats, coyotes, bobcats, and weasels

Tracks: The front tracks have four digits (toes), and the hind feet have five digits.

The Eastern Fox Squirrel is the largest tree squirrel in Michigan. It is gray or reddish brown with a yellowish or light-brown underside. Both the male and female look the same.

Did you know?

Michigan has the largest elk population east of the Mississippi. Elk are known to be the loudest of all cervids (deer family). Males produce a low-pitched bellow or roar, called a bugle. Bugling is a technique that involves both roaring and whistling at the same time. Elks use their bugle or bugling to attract mates or announce territories during the fall mating season. Their bugles can be heard over long distances.

Size Comparison   Most Active   Track Size

     4½"

Elk

Cervus elaphus canadensis

Size: 5–8 feet tall; weighs 377–1,095 pounds

Habitat: Open woodlands, mountain areas, shrublands, coniferous swamps, and hardwood forests

Range: Restricted to a few counties in northern Michigan

Food: Elk are herbivores that eat grasses; flowers; and leaves from trees like cedar, Red Maple, and basswood.

Den: No den; will lay in grass to rest. Mother elk will hide young calves in tall grasses.

Young: Calves are born between 240–265 days. At birth, calves weigh around 30 pounds and have spots through the first summer. Separation from mother's milk happens around the 60-day mark, but calves will continue to get care and protection from mom for around a year. They reach full maturity around 16 months, but males will usually wait to mate until they are older.

Predators: Cougars or mountain lions, Gray Wolves, and bears. Calves may fall victim to bobcats and coyotes.

Tracks: Front tracks of an adult are about 4¾ inches long and wide. Hind foot tracks are 4½ inches long and 3½ inches wide. Two toes are on both feet.

Elk come in different shades of browns and tans. In the summer and spring they are lighter brown to tan, while in the winter they are a deep dark brown; during both seasons, they have a cream or off-white rump. They sport a darker tone on the head, neck, belly, and legs.

Did you know?

All wolves in the United States (except the Red Wolf in the Southeast) are Gray Wolves! Each area has its own subspecies (a group that is a little different physically or genetically), and their common names are often based on their habitat. Gray Wolves are often referred to as Timberwolves.

Size Comparison   Most Active   Track Size

4⅝"

Gray Wolf

Canis lupus

Size: 5–6½ feet long; weighs 60–130 pounds

Habitat: Forests and grasslands

Range: Throughout the upper peninsula of Michigan and the Isle Royale National Park; wolves patrol territories that are 25–150 square miles.

Food: Deer; moose; elk; and smaller animals like rabbits, beavers, and birds. Sometimes wolves feed young (or pups) vegetation, such as blueberries.

Den: For the first couple of weeks, the alpha (lead) female stays with the pups to keep them warm and fed. During this time, she is totally dependent on the remainder of the pack to provide her with food. Once the pups are large enough to be alone, the female can leave them and hunt to support the growing pack.

Young: Pups are born in April or May; 4 to 7 pups are born at one time; they stay in the den for 6–8 weeks and eventually leave the pack at 1–2 years of age.

Predators: Bears, other wolves, coyotes (which prey on young wolves), and humans

Tracks: Front paws are around 5 inches long; hind paws are 4 inches long; both front and hind paws have a width of 3 to 3½ inches.

Gray Wolves can be gray, black, or even red. Wolves live in groups called packs. Packs can be as small as 2 wolves and as large as 13 or more. Wolves will hunt in packs; when hunts are successful, the whole pack will feed on the kill, with the alpha eating first.

Did you know?

Bats are the only mammals that can really fly. All other "flying" mammals use extra skin to glide through the air, while bats can use their wings to achieve lift, just like birds!

Size Comparison   Most Active   Hibernates

Little Brown Bat

Myotis lucifugus

Size: 3–4½ inches long; wingspan of 8–9 inches; weighs less than an ounce

Habitat: Wooded areas, caves, and suburban areas

Range: Found in most of Michigan, with higher numbers reported in the northern part of the state; also found throughout the United States and northern Mexico

Food: Flying insects like moths, beetles, and mosquitoes

Den: Bats den in groups called colonies; roosting sites are in hollow trees, caves, and even buildings. Bats roost in groups made of females and pups called maternity colonies.

Young: Females give birth to one pup, which will hang onto its mother; pups begin flying at 3 weeks.

Predators: Owls, snakes, raccoons, and outdoor cats

Tracks: Bats don't often leave tracks, but you can smell and see bat droppings (guano) in roosting sites.

The Little Brown Bat is a short-eared bat with dark-brown ears and snout; each fall, when temperatures drop, bats migrate to their favorite hibernation sites such as caves, tunnels, and wells. If you see a bat, don't touch it, but tell an adult; bats usually keep to themselves, so a bat spotted near people may be sick. Bats can sometimes be spotted outside, and those are often perfectly healthy.

The Little Brown Bat does not often leave tracks.

Did you know?

Weasels are small but tough! They will attack prey over three times their own size, and they help control rodent and pest species by eating mice, voles, and other small mammals.

Size Comparison   Most Active   Track Size

1¾"

Long-tailed Weasel
Mustela frenata

Size: 14–18 inches long; weighs 5 ounces to 1 pound

Habitat: Forests, farms, and rocky areas

Range: Weasels can be found throughout Michigan and the rest of the United States, except for a small pocket in southern California, Nevada, and Arizona

Food: Ducks, frogs, birds, rodents, rabbits, and sometimes domesticated chickens and eggs; they will hide extra food to eat later.

Den: Weasels will dig dens but will also use rock piles, abandoned burrows of other animals, or hollow logs. Dens are covered with fur and grass.

Young: 4–8 kits are born in April; they reach adult weight within 4 months.

Predators: Hawks, owls, coyotes, foxes, humans, and cats

Tracks: The front foot is wider than the hind foot. Both sets of feet have five toe pads with four claws extending from them.

Long-tailed Weasels have several color phases, including alternating from brown to white as the seasons change from summer to winter.

Did you know?

The Meadow Vole is the largest vole that is found in Michigan. When threatened, voles will stomp their hind feet like a rabbit does. A Meadow Vole can eat over 50% of its body weight per day.

Size Comparison   Most Active   Track Size

Meadow Vole

Microtus pennsylvanicus

Size: 5–7 inches long; weighs 1–2½ ounces

Habitat: Grasslands, swamps, meadows, marshes, woodlands, farmlands, and open woody areas

Range: They are found throughout Michigan, the northern US, and Canada.

Food: Seeds, grasses, fruit, leaves, and sedges (marsh plants)

Den: No dens; they will nest aboveground or in a shallow nest at or just below the ground.

Young: 4–6 offspring per litter; young are born blind and without fur. Female cares for young for 2 weeks; young reach reproductive maturity at around 5–6 weeks.

Predators: Owls, hawks, snakes, weasels, and foxes

Tracks: The front foot is smaller than the hind foot and has four toes; the hind foot is larger with five toes.

The Meadow Vole has dark-brown fur on the back with a white-to-silver underbelly. It has small ears and black eyes. Voles create tracks or runways in grass and snow. Voles help the environment because they provide help when they turn over the soil by digging, and their waste provides nutrients to the soil.

Did you know?
Mink have webbed feet like otters. Although they usually dive and swim short distances, mink can dive over 13 feet deep and swim for over 95 feet underwater, if necessary!

Size Comparison   Most Active   Track Size

1¾"

Mink
Mustela vison

Size: 16–27 inches long; weighs 1½–3½ pounds

Habitat: Wetland areas with dense vegetation near streams, lakes, and swamps

Range: They are found across Michigan as well as throughout most of the US and Canada.

Food: Fish, eggs, snakes, muskrats, farm animals, small mammals, and aquatic animals such as crayfish

Den: Their dens are near water, in holes in the ground, hollow logs, and old muskrat and beaver lodges; they will use grass or fur from prey as bedding.

Young: At birth, they weigh less than an ounce. 3–6 young, called kits, are born; they are mature at 1 year old.

Predators: Otters, birds of prey, coyotes, bobcats, internal parasites, and humans (who trap them for fur)

Tracks: Both the front and hind tracks resemble a gloved hand. Both the left and right tracks are seen parallel to each other because the mink often bound (leap) when moving. Tracks are usually seen near water.

A mostly nocturnal (active at night) animal, it has a shiny or glossy dark-brown coat that it keeps all year long. Mink usually have a white or pale-yellow chest patch or bib on the throat that sometimes extends to the stomach.

Did you know?

Moose belong to the deer family, and they are the largest members of the deer family in the world! They can rotate their ears 180 degrees. Moose can swim over 5 miles per hour for over 8 miles, and they can also run over 35 miles per hour. Moose will dive beneath the water of ponds and lakes to reach the plants at the bottom.

Size Comparison   Most Active   Track Size

4"

Moose

Alces alces

Size: 7–10 feet long; 5–6½ feet from the shoulder to the ground; weighs 750–1,200 pounds or more

Habitat: Forested areas, marshes, and swamps

Range: They can be found on Isle Royale and the upper peninsula of Michigan, as well as in Canada, Alaska, and the northern parts of the eastern US. There are also populations in Wyoming and Colorado.

Food: Leaves, bark, twigs, roots, and aquatic plants

Den: Like other deer, moose dig out beds amid the forest floor.

Young: 1–2 young (calves) that are 25–35 pounds at birth; moose are considered adults at around 2 years old.

Predators: Bears, wolves, coyotes, and humans

Tracks: Hoofprints are large and heart-shaped.

Moose are a deep brown with a hump on the shoulder and a dewlap (a flap of skin) hanging down from the throat area. Males are larger than females, and they have large, flat antlers that can be over 4 feet wide and weigh over 30 pounds.

Did you know?

A single porcupine can have over 30,000 quills that they can use to protect themselves from predators. Porcupine quills are hollow and can be over 2 inches long. Porcupines are herbivores (plant eaters), and they have a special bacteria in their digestive system to help them break down the plant material.

Size Comparison   Most Active   Track Size

3⅜"

North American Porcupine

Erethizon dorsatum

Size: 2–3 feet long; weighs 10–25 pounds

Habitat: Forested areas, grasslands, and deserts

Range: They are found in the upper peninsula and the northern parts of the lower peninsula; they are also found throughout Canada and various areas across the northern and western US.

Food: Skunk cabbage, clovers, twigs, leaves, and tree bark

Den: They den in hollow logs and tree cavities.

Young: One young (porcupette) is born between May and July; they weigh a pound at birth and have 1-inch quills.

Predators: Lynx, bobcats, coyotes, owls, and fishers

Tracks: The front foot is shorter than the hind foot; the hind foot has five toes, while the front only has four toes.

The North American Porcupine is mostly nocturnal; its fur is black to gray and shades of brown with obvious quills. A porcupine has over 30,000 quills on its body; when threatened, it will turn around and strike an attacker with its tail quills, which are 4 inches long and are like needles. With that many quills, porcupines sometimes accidentally poke themselves. To protect itself (from itself), the porcupine has a special substance on its quills that acts like an antibiotic (or medicine). This prevents it from getting infected after an accidental poke. Like other mammals, porcupines need salt and will chew on, or lick, objects with the mineral to fulfill that craving. Sometimes this leads to porcupines chewing on human-made structures.

Did you know?

The raccoon is great at catching fish and other aquatic animals, such as mussels and crayfish. They are also excellent swimmers but usually avoid swimming because the water makes their fur heavy. Raccoons can turn their feet 180 degrees; this helps them when climbing, especially when going head-first down trees.

Size Comparison   Most Active   Track Size   Hibernates

3"

z^z

Northern Raccoon

Procyon lotor

Size: 24–40 inches long; weighs 15–28 pounds

Habitat: Woody areas, grasslands, suburban and urban areas, wetlands, and marshes

Range: They are found throughout Michigan and the US; they are also found in Mexico and southern Canada.

Food: Eggs, insects, garbage, garden plants, berries, nuts, and aquatic invertebrates like crayfish and mussels

Den: Raccoon dens are built in hollow trees, abandoned burrows, caves, and human-made structures.

Young: 2–6 young (kits) are born around March through July. They are born weighing 2 ounces, are around 4 inches long, and are blind with lightly colored fur.

Predators: Coyotes, foxes, bobcats, humans, and large birds of prey

Tracks: Their tracks resemble human handprints.

The Northern Raccoon has dense fur with variations of brown, black, and white streaks. It has a black mask on its face and a black-and-gray/brownish ringed tail. During the fall, it will grow a thick layer of fat to aid in staying warm through the winter.

Did you know?

Otters are good swimmers and can close their nostrils while diving. This allows them to dive for as long as 8 minutes and to depths of over 50 feet. Otter fur is the thickest of all mammal fur. River otters have an incredible 57,000 hairs for every square centimeter!

Size Comparison   Most Active   Track Size

3"

Northern River Otter

Lontra canadensis

Size: 29–48 inches long; weighs 10–33 pounds

Habitat: Lakes, marshes, rivers, and large streams; suburban areas

Range: Otters can be found throughout Michigan; they are also found along the US East and West Coasts, in Alaska, and in Canada.

Food: Fish, frogs, snakes, crabs, crawfish, mussels, birds, eggs, and turtles. They sometimes eat aquatic vegetation too.

Den: They den in burrows along the river, usually under rocks, riverbanks, hollow trees, and vegetation.

Young: 2–4 young (pups) are born between November and May. Pups are born with their eyes closed. They will leave the birthing area at around 6 months old and reach full maturity at around 2 or 3 years.

Predators: Alligators, coyotes, raptors, bobcats, bears, and dogs

Tracks: Their feet have nonretractable claws and are webbed.

Northern River Otters have thick, dark-brown fur with a long, slender body. Their fur is made up of two types: a short undercoat and a coarse topcoat that repels water. They have webbed feet and a layer of fat that helps keep them warm in cold water.

Did you know?

The Red Fox is a great jumper and can leap over 13 feet in one bound. Red foxes are also fast, as they can run up to 30 miles per hour. Red Foxes, like wild cats, will hide their food to eat later, often under leaf litter or in holes.

Size Comparison   Most Active   Track Size

2¼"

Red Fox

Vulpes vulpes

Size: 37–42 inches long; weighs 8–15 pounds

Habitat: Grasslands, forest edges, farm fields, and suburban areas

Range: Foxes are common throughout Michigan; they can be found throughout the eastern US and some parts of the Pacific Northwest.

Food: Omnivores (they eat both meat and plants); they eat frogs, birds, snakes, small mammals, insects, seeds, nuts, and fruit.

Den: They dig underground dens, sometimes several at once, splitting a litter (babies) between the two. They also use old badger or groundhog holes or tree roots for den sites.

Young: 3–7 young (kits) are born; pups will nurse (drink milk from the mother) for around 10 weeks and will become independent at around 7 months.

Predators: Coyotes, lynx, cougars, and other species of carnivores. Humans trap and hunt foxes for fur.

Tracks: Their footprints resemble dog tracks with four toe pads; they walk in a line with the hind foot behind the front.

The Red Fox is a medium-size predator with a burnt orange or rust-like red coat with a bushy, white-tipped tail. The legs are usually black or grayish. The Red Fox's tail is actually longer than its body.

Did you know?
Snowshoe hares can run over 20 miles per hour and can jump over 8 feet in a single leap. Their name comes from their hind feet, which are large and furry and look (and act) like snowshoes.

Size Comparison   Most Active   Track Size

4–5"

Snowshoe Hare

Lepus americanus

Size: 17–22 inches long; tail is 2 inches long; weighs 3–4½ pounds

Habitat: Woody areas, swamps, open fields, and forest bogs

Range: They are found in the Upper Peninsula and the north-central areas of the Lower Peninsula of Michigan, the northern US into the Appalachian Mountains, and on the Pacific Coast.

Food: Grasses, flowers, bark, twigs, evergreen needles; they sometimes will eat the remains of other snowshoe hares.

Den: None

Young: They give birth to 2–4 young (known as leverets); during the day, young will hide in different places and will only come together with the mother to nurse (drink milk) for a few short minutes. Young are mature one year after birth.

Predators: Bobcats, coyotes, mink, foxes, owls, and other birds of prey

Tracks: Their hind feet are larger than the front.

The Snowshoe Hare is a medium-size, rabbit-like animal with brown fur in the summer and a white coat in the winter. They are mostly active during the dawn and dusk hours of the day (crepuscular).

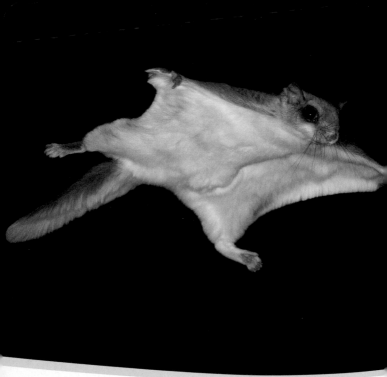

Did you know?

The Southern Flying Squirrel doesn't actually fly! Instead, it uses special folds of skin to glide through the air. They can glide over 100 feet at a time. They have thick paws that aid them in landing. Because they move from tree to tree, they help to spread seeds and fungi.

Size Comparison   Most Active

Southern Flying Squirrel

Glaucomys volans

Size: 9 inches long; weighs 2–3 ounces

Habitat: Forests with older trees

Range: They are found in central Michigan and southward to the state line and throughout the eastern US and parts of Mexico.

Food: Nuts, berries, acorns, small birds, mice, insects, and mushrooms

Den: They make nests in tree hollows. They will also use abandoned woodpecker holes and human-made nest boxes or birdhouses. They line the nest with chewed bark, grasses, moss, and feathers.

Young: 2–3 young (kittens) are born per litter; they drink milk from the mother for around 70 days and will be fully independent around 4 months and mature at around a year old.

Predators: Small hawks, foxes, owls, martens (weasel-like mammals), and weasels

Tracks: Their tracks are seldom seen due to their gliding nature.

The Southern Flying Squirrel is a grayish-brown nocturnal (active at night) animal that glides through the air from tree to tree. The patagium, or skin fold, stretches from their ankles to their wrist, allowing them to "fly." (People have even built similar "squirrel suits" to glide with, and they've worked!) During winter months, flying squirrels share cavities with others.

Did you know?

The opossum is the only marsupial native to the US. Marsupials are a special group of animals that are most well known for their pouches, which they use to carry their young. When frightened, young opossums will play dead (called playing possum) and adults will show their teeth and hiss or run away.

Size Comparison   Most Active   Track Size

2½"

Virginia Opossum

Didelphis virginiana

Size: 22–45 inches long; weighs 4–8 pounds

Habitat: Forests, woodlands, meadows, and suburban areas

Range: They are found throughout Michigan, except the far northern portion and upper peninsula; they are found throughout the eastern US, Canada, and also in Mexico and Costa Rica.

Food: Eggs, garbage, insects, worms, birds, fruit, and occasionally small reptiles and amphibians

Den: They den in hollow trees, abandoned animal burrows, and buildings.

Young: A litter of 6–20 young (joeys) are born blind and without fur; their limbs are not fully formed. Young will climb from the birthing area into the mother's pouch and stay until 8 weeks old; they then alternate between the mother's pouch and her back for 4 weeks. At 12 weeks they are independent.

Predators: Hawks, owls, pet cats and dogs, coyotes, and bobcats

Tracks: The front feet are 2 inches long and around 1½ inches wide and resemble a child's hands; the hind feet are 2½ inches long and around 2¼ inches wide; they have fingers in front with a fifth finger that acts as a thumb.

The Virginia Opossum has long gray-and-black fur; the face is white, and the tail is pink to pale and furless. Possums have long claws.

Did you know?

When they first emerge, a deer's antlers are covered in a special skin called velvet. Deer can run up to 40 miles per hour and can jump over 8 feet vertically (high) and over 15 feet horizontally (long).

Size Comparison   Most Active   Track Size

3"

White-tailed Deer

Odocoileus virginianus

Size: 4–6 feet long; 3–4 feet tall at front shoulder; weighs 114–308 pounds

Habitat: Forest edges, brushy fields, woody farmlands, prairies, and swamps

Range: They are found throughout Michigan and throughout the US except for much of the Southwest; they are also found in southern Canada and into South America.

Food: Fruits, grass, tree shrubs, nuts, and bark

Den: Deer do not den but will bed down in tall grasses and shrub areas.

Young: Deer usually give birth to twins (fawns) that are 3–6 pounds in late May to June. The fawns are born with spots; this coloration helps them hide in vegetation. Young become independent at 1–2 years.

Predators: Wolves, coyotes, bears, bobcats, and humans

Tracks: Both front and hind feet have two teardrop- or comma-shaped toes.

Crepuscular (active at dawn and dusk), White-tailed Deer have big brown eyes with eye rings and a long snout with a black, glossy nose. The males have antlers, which fall off each year. All deer have a white tail that they flash upward when alarmed. Deer molt or change fur color twice a year. They sport a rusty-brown fur in the summer; in early fall, they transition to winter coats that are grayish brown in color.

Did you know?

The Wolverine is the largest member of the weasel family that lives on land. Wolverines will spray their food stash with a funky odor to prevent other animals from stealing it. Some people call them "Skunk Bears" due to their bear-like movement and pattern that resembles a skunk. They are small but mighty animals, about as big as a medium-size dog, and they can take down animals over three times their size.

Size Comparison   Most Active   Track Size

3½—7"

Wolverine
Gulo gulo

Size: 31–46 inches long; weighs 20–50 pounds

Habitat: Remote forests, grasslands, and rocky areas

Range: Once found in several areas of Michigan, wolverines haven't been recorded in the state in decades, aside from a solitary female in 2004 in Ann Arbor that was confirmed dead. Other wolverines are rumored to still live in the area. They can be found in Alaska, the northern US, and Canada.

Food: Omnivores; bird eggs, reindeer, wild sheep, elk, rodents, and rabbits

Den: Sleeping dens are found in natural hollowed-out areas, including caves, fallen trees, and crevices. Females will make birth dens in snow that is 5 or more feet deep.

Young: 3 kits are born at a time. They are born blind and weigh less than a pound. Kits are weaned off the mother's milk at around 3 months. Kits can find food on their own at around 7 months.

Predators: Wolverines do not have many natural predators.

Tracks: Front tracks are 3½–5½ inches long and 3½–4 inches wide. Hind tracks are 3½–7 inches long and 3¼–5½ inches wide.

Wolverines are thick-bodied or husky animals with brown or black base fur with a golden or yellowish stripe that extends from their head down to their bottom. Each individual has its own unique stripe pattern (much like a fingerprint).

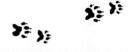

Did you know?

Woodchucks are important parts of the ecosystem. Their abandoned burrows are used by several other types of wildlife, including foxes, weasels, skunks, and possums. Whistle pig is another common name for woodchucks; this is because they make a high-pitched whistle sound when alarmed, alerting nearby groundhogs of danger.

Size Comparison   Most Active   Track Size   Hibernates

Woodchuck (Groundhog)

Marmota monax

Size: 21½–30 inches long; weighs 6–11 pounds

Habitat: Forest edges, rocky areas, and meadows

Range: They are found throughout Michigan, as well as in much of the eastern US and into parts of the South.

Food: Wild grasses, berries, insects, baby birds, and farm crops; groundhogs also feast on gardens.

Den: They build summer and winter dens that have multiple entrances.

Young: 4–6 kits are born in late April to early May; groundhogs are independent at 2 months and adults at 1 year old.

Predators: Red Foxes, coyotes, Black Bears, snakes, hawks, and bobcats

Tracks: The front feet are 1¾ inches long, with four digits resembling fingers; the hind feet are 2 inches long with five digits.

A Woodchuck is a large brown rodent that has two layers of waterproof fur. This fur helps them to stay warm in the winter and helps them dry quickly after being in the water. Groundhogs eat a lot of food in the summer and survive the winter by using the excess fat they build up.

Did you know?

The American Goldfinch helps restore habitats by spreading seeds. The goldfinch gets its color from a pigment called a carotenoid (say it, cuh-rot-en-oid) in the seeds it eats. It can even feed upside down by using its feet to bring seeds to its mouth.

Nest Type

Migrates

American Goldfinch

Spinus tristis

Size: 4½–5 inches long; wingspan of 9 inches; weighs about half an ounce

Habitat: Grasslands, meadows, suburban areas, and wetlands

Range: Found throughout most of Michigan year-round; in summer, they can be found in far northern parts of the state; found all over the US

Food: Seeds of plants and trees; sometimes feeds on insects; loves thistle seeds at birdfeeders

Nesting: Goldfinches build a nest in late June.

Nest: Cup-shaped nests are built a couple of feet above-ground out of branches and twigs.

Eggs: 2–7 eggs with a bluish-white tint

Young: Young (chicks) hatch around 15 days after being laid; they hatch without feathers and weigh only a gram. Chicks learn to fly after around 11–15 days. Young become mature at around 11 months old.

Predators: Garter Snakes, Blue Jays, American Kestrels, and cats

Migration: Most goldfinches stay in Michigan for the winter, though birds in the northern part of the state migrate south.

During the summer, American Goldfinch males are brightly colored with golden-yellow feathers and an orange beak. They have black wings with white wing bars. The crown (top) of the head is black. In winter, they molt, and the males look more like the females. Females are always brown with hints of yellow around the head area.

Did you know?

The American Redstart will use its tail to scare its prey. The American Redstart pops or flicks the red patches on its wings and tail, which causes the insect to be startled and fly up. The Redstart then grabs the insect.

Nest Type

Migrates

American Redstart

Setophaga ruticilla

Size: 4¼–5½ inches long; wingspan of 6¼–7½ inches; weighs around ¼ ounce

Habitat: Forests and shrubby areas

Range: During breeding season, they can be found throughout Michigan. In winter, they are found in central and northern South America.

Food: Omnivores that feed on moths, caterpillars, and beetles. They will also eat berries and fruits.

Nesting: Females build a cup-shaped nest in trees on the main branch of the trunk. They will also nest in shrubs.

Nest: Cup-shaped nest made of plant fibers like grasses, leaves, bark, and pine needles

Eggs: 1–5 eggs; white or creamy with blotches of brown or red; some are so speckled they are nearly all brown.

Young: Eggs hatch 10–12 days after laying. Chicks are born with eyes closed and are almost featherless besides a few downy feathers. Around 8–14 days after hatching, they will leave the nest.

Predators: Snakes, squirrels, owls, Common Ravens, Blue Jays, Red-bellied Woodpeckers, and a variety of hawks

Migration: In fall, they migrate south from Michigan to northern South America, making stops in the southern United States and Central America. In spring, they migrate north from South America to Michigan.

Males are black with vibrant orange to reddish spots on the sides of their bodies, wings, and tails. Juveniles and females are a grayish to olive brown with yellow patches or spots.

Did you know?

American Robins have a great sense of hearing. They hunt for earthworms underground using only their hearing. Robins are opportunistic feeders in urban (city) areas; they will wait for lawns to be disturbed by mowers, sprinklers, or rain, and then feed on the worms that have emerged. The American Robin is the state bird of Michigan!

Nest Type

American Robin

Turdus migratorius

Size: 9–11 inches long; wingspan of 17 inches; weighs 2½–3 ounces

Habitat: Cities, forests, and lawns

Range: They can be found throughout most of Michigan year-round, and during the breeding season they can be found in the far northern parts of the state, including the Upper Peninsula and throughout North America except the extreme north of Canada.

Food: Fruit, earthworms, beetle grubs, caterpillars

Nesting: April to July

Nest: Cup-shaped nests are exclusively built by the female 5–14 feet off the ground in bushes or trees. Nests are constructed of grass, paper, twigs, and feathers. A new nest is built for each set of eggs.

Eggs: 3–5 sky-blue eggs

Young: Eggs hatch after 14 days of incubation; chicks hatch blind and without feathers. Hatchlings (chicks) leave the nest after 2 weeks but will continue to beg for food from parents.

Predators: Snakes, crows, cats, foxes, raccoons, squirrels, raptors, and weasels

Migration: The majority of birds stay throughout the winter, while some in the Upper Peninsula migrate south to warmer areas.

American Robin males have a dark black-to-gray head with a brown back, a rusty-orange chest, and white eye circles. Females are similar in color but are not as bright as the male, and they usually have a brownish head.

Did you know?

The Bald Eagle is an endangered species success story! The Bald Eagle was once endangered due to a pesticide called DDT that weakened eggshells and caused them to crack early. Through the banning of DDT and other conservation efforts, the Bald Eagle population recovered, and it was removed from the Endangered Species List in July of 2007.

Nest Type

Bald Eagle

Haliaeetus leucocephalus

Size: 3½ feet long; wingspan of 6½–8 feet; weighs 8–14 pounds

Habitat: Forests and tree stands (small forests) near river edges, lakes, seashores, and wetlands

Range: They are a resident bird throughout Michigan; they are found throughout much of the US.

Food: Fish, waterfowl (ducks), rabbits, squirrels, muskrats, and deer carcasses; will steal food from other eagles or osprey

Nesting: Eagles have lifelong partners that begin nesting in early fall.

Nest: They build a large nest at the tops of trees out of sticks; the nest can be over 5 feet wide and over 6 feet tall, often shaped like an upside-down cone.

Eggs: 1–3 white eggs

Young: Young (chicks) will hatch around 35 days; young will leave the nest around 12 weeks. It takes up to 5 years for eagles to get that iconic look!

Predators: Few; collisions with cars sometimes occur.

Migration: They are short-distance migrators, usually to coastal areas; in Michigan, many eagles do not migrate at all nor do they leave the state.

Adult Bald Eagles have a dark-brown body, a white head and tail, and a golden-yellow beak. Juvenile eagles are dark brown with a couple of white feathers on the wings and tail. A Bald Eagle can use its wings as oars to propel itself across bodies of water.

Did you know?
The Barred Owl has a different eye color from all other Michigan owls; it has brown eyes, while the others all have yellow ones! Barred Owls, like other owls, have special structures on their primary feathers that allow them to fly silently through the air.

Nest Type

Barred Owl
Strix varia

Size: 17–20 inches long; wingspan of 3½ feet; weighs 2 pounds

Habitat: Forested areas, near flood plains of lakes and rivers

Range: They can be found throughout the state of Michigan; they are found throughout the eastern US and southern Canada, with scattered populations throughout the Pacific Northwest.

Food: Squirrels, rabbits, and mice; will also prey on birds and aquatic animals like frogs, fish, and crayfish

Nesting: Starts in March

Nest: They use hollow trees; they will also use abandoned nests of other animals and human-made nest structures.

Eggs: 2–4 white eggs with a rough shell

Young: Young (chicks) hatch between 27 and 33 days; they have white down feathers and leave the nest around 5 weeks after hatching. They are fully independent at around 6 months and fully mature at around 2 years.

Predators: Great Horned Owls, raccoons, weasels, and sometimes Northern Goshawks feed on eggs and young in the nest.

Migration: Barred Owls do not migrate, but their range is expanding in the Pacific Northwest.

The Barred Owl is a medium-size bird with dark rings highlighting the face. Their feathers are brown and grayish, often with streaking or a bar-like pattern. They have no ear tufts and have a rounded head with a yellow beak and brown eyes. They can easily be identified by their call: "Who cooks for you, who cooks for you all?"

Did you know?

Kingfishers inspired human technology! Bullet trains around the world are designed after the Kingfisher's beak, which allows them to dive into water without a splash. This design was used in bullet trains to allow them to enter into tunnels without making a large booming sound. This process of modeling human technology after animal features is called biomimicry.

Nest Type   Migrates

72

Belted Kingfisher

Megaceryle alcyon

Size: 11–13¾ inches long; wingspan is 19–24 inches; weighs 5–6 ounces

Habitat: Forest and grassland areas near rivers, ponds, lakes

Range: Resident throughout most of Michigan; can be found in northern parts of both peninsulas in summer

Food: Carnivore; mostly fish and other aquatic animals such as crayfish and frogs, and occasionally other birds, mammals, and berries

Nesting: Nests are in the form of upward-sloped burrows that are dug in soft banks on or near water. (The upward slopes prevent flooding.)

Nest: Nests are in the form of upward-slopped burrows that are dug in soft banks on or near water.

Eggs: 5–8 white, smooth, glossy eggs are laid per brood (group of eggs).

Young: Chicks are born featherless with pink skin, closed eyes, and a dark bill. They receive care from both parents. Chicks leave the nest after about 28 days.

Predators: Snakes, hawks, and mammals

Migration: Mostly a resident bird; in some areas, will migrate south during non-breeding season

The Belted Kingfisher is bluish gray on top; the bottom half is white with a blue/gray belt or band. The wings have white spots on them. Unlike most other birds, the Kingfisher female has a different pattern than the male. Females have a reddish-brown or rusty-orange band on their stomachs.

Did you know?

Black-capped Chickadees have a unique strategy for surviving winter. The area of the brain that aids in memory (the hippocampus) temporarily gets bigger in preparation for winter. This allows them to remember where they hid or cached seeds.

Nest Type

Black-capped Chickadee

Poecile atricapillus

Size: 5½–7½ inches long; wingspan of 8 inches; weighs about half an ounce

Habitat: Forests, woodland edges, and urban areas

Range: They are year-round residents of Michigan and can be found in the northern United States.

Food: Caterpillars, insects, seeds, spiders, and berries

Nesting: April to August

Nest: Chickadees utilize old woodpecker nests or make their own cup-shaped nests in trees that have been weakened by rot.

Eggs: 6–8 eggs that are white with brown spots

Young: 12–13 days after laying, eggs hatch and chicks will leave the nest at around 15 days; chickadee parents will leave the nest with the young and continue feeding for another 5–6 weeks.

Predators: Hawks, owls, shrikes, raccoons, house cats left outside, and other mammals

Migration: They do not migrate.

A Black-capped Chickadee has a gray body with a black cap, or top of head, and a black throat and beak; they have white cheeks and light bellies.

Did you know?

Blue Jays can mimic; they have been known to copy human speech and often fool birders by mimicking hawks. Blue Jays get the name "jay" from their nosy and rambunctious personality. Sometimes Blue Jays will mimic hawk calls to scare birds into dropping food. Other possible explanations include using the call to warn other birds that a hawk may be nearby.

Nest Type

Blue Jay

Cyanocitta cristata

Size: 11–12½ inches long; wingspan of 16 inches; weighs 2½–3½ ounces

Habitat: Forests and forest edges, suburban areas, city parks, and farm fields

Range: They can be found throughout the state of Michigan; their range extends from northeastern through central Canada and the edges of southwestern states like Arizona and Nebraska.

Food: Acorns, seeds, insects, fruits, eggs, nuts, and other birds after they die

Nesting: March to July

Nest: The gathering of nesting materials and the building of nests are shared by both male and female; a cup-shaped nest is built in the fork of tree branches.

Eggs: 4–5 eggs that are either blue or light brown and speckled with brown spots

Young: Chicks hatch naked with eyes closed around 17 days after eggs are laid. Nestlings are cared for by both parents and usually leave the nest 17–20 days after hatching.

Predators: Snakes, crows, falcons, owls, cats, raccoons, and hawks

Migration: Most stay in the area they are found in, but some will migrate south.

The Blue Jay's upper body feathers are made up of different shades of blue and black, and it has a blue crest (feathers on its head); the underbody is white or gray. A Blue Jay can hold food items with its feet and use its beak to open them. Sometimes they will store food for later.

Did you know?

Canada Geese sometimes travel over 600 miles in a day. They fly in a V formation, which allows them to travel long distances without stopping because they can switch positions. As the lead bird gets tired, it drops to the back of the line and a new bird leads. The V formation helps them communicate and helps prevent collisions.

Nest Type   Migrates

Canada Goose

Branta canadensis

Size: 2–3½ feet long; wingspan of 5–6 feet; weighs 6½–20 pounds

Habitat: Ponds, marshes, lakes, parks, and farm fields

Range: They can be found throughout Michigan as residents; they are widespread in the rest of the US.

Food: Insects, aquatic (growing in the water) plants, skunk cabbage, seeds, berries, grasses, and farm crops like soybeans

Nesting: March to April

Nest: Nests are made on the ground, on elevated areas near the water, or sometimes on a muskrat mound. Nest sites are picked with protection in mind; areas that have clear views and vantage points are more likely to be used.

Eggs: 2–8 cream-colored eggs that are 3 inches long and about 2½ inches wide

Young: Goslings hatch about a month after being laid. They are born with yellow down feathers that they lose as they get older. At the time of hatching, they can swim and walk.

Predators: Mink, raccoons, foxes, dogs, and Great Horned Owls

Migration: A large portion will stay and winter in Michigan, while others will fly farther south.

The Canada Goose is recognizable by its famous honk and body pattern of brown feathers with a black neck, head, bill, and even feet. They have white cheek feathers.

Did you know?

Because of the way their legs are situated on their body, loons aren't good at walking on land. Loons have to get a running (or swimming) start to take off from the water.

Nest Type   Migrates

Common Loon

Gavia immer

Size: 28–36 inches long; wingspan of 40–55 inches; weighs 3½–13 pounds

Habitat: Quiet freshwater lakes, coastal waters, and woody lakes

Range: They can be found throughout northern Michigan during breeding seasons and southern parts of Michigan as a migrant; they're found in several other northern states and in Canada.

Food: Fish, insects, snails, and crayfish

Nesting: May to July

Nest: The male selects the nesting spot; males and females will build the clump nest together near the water.

Eggs: 2 eggs that have a brown base layer with brown spots

Young: Young (adorably called loonlets) usually hatch in 29 days, covered with dark, fuzzy down; they can swim immediately after hatching. Chicks will ride on their parent's back.

Predators: Mink, raccoons, skunks, and eagles

Migration: Loons migrate to southern states.

The Common Loon sports a black-and-white checkered back and a dark green-and-blackish head with red eyes and a black bill. During the fall, adults lose their checkered spots and have a plain back.

Did you know?

Bluebirds are not really blue! The "blue" that we see is visible because of the way that light hits the structure of the feathers, but there is no blue pigment in their feathers. The Eastern Bluebird will use a large variety of sounds to attract a mate; sometimes upwards to 1,000 songs will be used.

Nest Type

Migrates

Eastern Bluebird
Sialia sialis

Size: 7 inches long; wingspan of 13 inches; weighs 1 ounce

Habitat: Open woodlands, meadows, prairies, gardens, parks, and suburban areas

Range: They can be found in the entire state of Michigan and throughout the eastern and southern United States.

Food: Berries, insects, and seeds

Nesting: Late March to late July or early August

Nest: Bluebirds utilize woodpecker cavities and other tree holes, as well as nesting boxes. The nest is lined with feathers and grasses.

Eggs: Clutch (group of eggs) size is 4–5; eggs are a light blue color.

Young: Chicks hatch featherless and blind. They gain sight in 1 week and have all feathers around 2 weeks. Chicks will leave the nest around 3 weeks but receive care until about 4 weeks.

Predators: House Sparrows and European Starlings will invade nests and destroy eggs.

Migration: They migrate to the southern United States.

Eastern Bluebird males are a rich blue with a rusty breast; females are a dull brown with faint blue feathers. Bluebirds are known to return to Michigan in February.

Did you know?

The Eastern and Western Meadowlarks look almost exactly the same. A few ways to tell them apart are that the Western Meadowlark is a little less vibrant in color and has a different song. The Western Meadowlark can be also found in groups or flocks more often than the Eastern.

Nest Type

Migrates

Eastern Meadowlark/
Western Meadowlark

Sturnella magna/Sturnella neglecta

Size: Eastern: 7½–10 inches long; wingspan of 14–16 inches; weighs 3–5 ounces; Western: 6–10 inches long; wingspan of 14–16 inches; weighs 3–4 ounces

Habitat: Eastern: farm fields, grasslands, and wet fields; Western: pastures, native grasslands, and farm fields

Range: Found throughout Michigan during the breeding season. Eastern Meadowlarks are found in the eastern portion of the country; Western Meadowlarks are found to the west.

Food: Mostly insects and other soft-bodied invertebrates

Nesting: Males select a territory in March. When females arrive a couple of weeks later, they select a mate after going through an air courtship display.

Nest: Female builds a cup-shaped depression in the ground.

Eggs: Eastern: 3–5 white eggs with purple and brown spots. Western: 3–7 white eggs with purple and brown spots.

Young: Female birds incubate the eggs for 13–16 days; chicks hatch with eyes closed and naked, with pink-orange skin and a few gray down feathers present. They receive care from both parents and will fledge (leave) the nest around 10 days or so.

Predators: Domestic cats, foxes, dogs, skunks, coyotes, raptors

Migration: In fall, they migrate south; they return in spring.

Meadowlarks have a striped brown head and upper half, and a gray bill. They have a yellow underside with their breast adorned by a black "V."

Did you know?

The Great Blue Heron is the largest and most common heron species. A heron's eye color changes as it ages. The eyes start out gray but transition to yellow over time. Great Blue Herons swallow prey whole.

Nest Type

Migrates

Great Blue Heron

Ardea herodias

Size: 3–4½ feet long; wingspan of 6–7 feet; weighs 5–7 pounds

Habitat: Lakes, ponds, rivers, marshes, lagoons, wetlands, and coastal areas like beaches

Range: They can be found throughout Michigan, as well as the entire United States and down into Mexico.

Food: Fish, rats, crabs, shrimp, grasshoppers, crayfish, other birds, snakes, and lizards

Nesting: March to May

Nest: 2–3 feet across and saucer shaped; often grouped in large rookeries (colonies) in tall trees along the water's edge. Nests are built out of sticks and are often located in dead trees more than 100 feet above the ground; nests are used year after year.

Eggs: 3–7 pale bluish eggs

Young: Chicks will hatch after 28 days of incubation; young will stay in the nest for around 10 weeks. They reach reproductive maturity at just under 2 months.

Predators: Eagles, crows, gulls, raccoons, bears, hawks, and Turkey Vultures

Migration: Populations in northern areas will fly south to southern states, the Caribbean, and Central America.

The Great Blue Heron is a large wading bird with blue and gray upper body feathers; the stomach area is white. They have long yellow legs that they use to stalk prey in the water. When out of the water, they will spread their feet out and balance themselves to hunt creatures in the water below.

Did you know?

A Great Horned Owl can exert a crushing force of over 300 pounds with its talons. The Great Horned Owl's "horns" are not horns at all. They are not made of bone-like material, and in fact, they aren't even ears! They are tufts made of feathers, and they help an owl stay hidden by allowing it to resemble tree branches and bark.

Nest Type

Great Horned Owl

Bubo virginianus

Size: Up to 23 inches long; wingspan of 45 inches; weighs 3 pounds

Habitat: Woods; swamps; desert edges; as well as heavily populated areas such as cities, suburbs, and parks

Range: They are found throughout Michigan and the continent of North America.

Food: They eat a variety of foods, but mostly mammals. Sometimes they eat other birds as well.

Nesting: They have lifelong partnerships, with nesting season starting in early winter; egg-laying starts in mid-January to February.

Nest: Nests are found 20–50 feet off the ground. They tend to reuse nests from other raptors or hollowed-out trees.

Eggs: The female lays 2–4 whitish eggs at a time. Eggs are incubated for around 30 days.

Young: Young can fly at around 9 weeks old. The parents care for and feed young for several months.

Predators: Young owls are preyed upon by foxes, coyotes, bears, and opossums. As adults, they are rarely attacked by other birds of prey, such as Golden Eagles and Goshawks.

Migration: Great Horned Owls are not regular migrators, but some individuals will travel south during the winter.

They are bulky birds with large ear tufts, a rusty brown-to-grayish face with a black border, and large bright eyes. The body color tends to be brown; the wing pattern is checkered with an intermingled dark brown. The chest and belly areas are light brown and have white bars.

Did you know?

The Green-winged Teal is the smallest of the dabbling ducks that are native to America. They can reach speeds up to 60 miles per hour (mph). Teals will dive underwater to avoid predators.

Nest Type   Migrates

Green-winged Teal

Anas crecca carolinensis

Size: 13–16 inches long; wingspan of 20–23 inches; weighs 5 ounces–1 pound

Habitat: Wetlands and ponds

Range: This bird breeds in a few northern states, including Michigan, as well as northern Canada and Alaska. They will spend winter in the southern United States.

Food: Seeds, plant stems, aquatic vegetation, insects, maggots, and mollusks

Nesting: April to May

Nest: Females build a bowl-shaped nest in high aquatic vegetation like grasses and cattails.

Eggs: 5–16 creamy white eggs

Young: Chicks hatch around 20–23 days after eggs are laid. Chicks can swim the same day they hatch. They usually reach reproductive maturity at 1 year.

Predators: Humans, eagles, Red Foxes, Striped Skunks, crows, and Black-billed Magpies

Migration: They migrate south in the fall and winter, and north during spring migration

Green-winged Teals are small ducks with a short, stout body. Adult males have gray-and-brown lined bodies with a cinnamon-brown head and a white streak at the midsection of the body. A green swoosh extends from the eye to the back of the head. Females are brown. Both males and females have a green wing spot.

Did you know?

Hairy and Downy Woodpeckers are the smallest woodpecker species in North America, with the Downy being the smallest of all woodpeckers. Hairy Woodpeckers can hear insects traveling under the tree bark. Downy Woodpeckers have a built-in mask, or special feathers, near their nostrils that helps them to avoid breathing in woodchips while pecking.

Nest Type

Hairy/Downy Woodpecker

Leuconotopicus villosus/Dryobates pubescens

Size: Hairy: 7–10 inches long; wingspan of 13–16 inches; weighs 3 ounces; Downy: 5½–7 inches long; wingspan of 10–12 inches; weighs less than an ounce

Habitat: Forested areas, parks, woodlands, and orchards

Range: Throughout Michigan and across the United States

Food: Hairy: beetles, ants, caterpillars, fruits, and seeds; Downy: beetles, ants, galls, wasps, seeds, and berries

Nesting: Hairy: March to June; Downy: January to March

Nest: In both woodpecker species, pairs will work together to create a cavity. Both parents also help to incubate eggs.

Eggs: Hairy: 4 white eggs; Downy: 3–8 white eggs

Young: Hairy Woodpeckers' eggs will hatch 2 weeks after being laid and then fledge (develop enough feathers to fly) after another month. Downy Woodpeckers' eggs will hatch after about 12 days and fledge 18–21 days after hatching. Both species are born blind and featherless.

Predators: American Kestrels, snakes, Sharp-shinned Hawks, domesticated cats, rats, squirrels, and Cooper's Hawks

Migration: Woodpeckers are mostly year-round residents, but some in the north may travel south during the winter.

Hairy Woodpeckers and Downy Woodpeckers look strikingly similar with their color pattern. One way to distinguish them is to look at the size of the body and bill. The Downy Woodpecker is smaller than the Hairy Woodpecker and has a shorter bill. If you look at the tail feathers of the two species, you will also see that the Hairy Woodpecker does not have white spots, while the Downy's tail does.

Did you know?

Groups of Hooded Mergansers will avoid being attacked by raptors by mimicking the shape of a swimming muskrat. The merganser is the only duck species that is a fish-eating specialist; it can dive underwater for up to two minutes while fishing.

Nest Type   Migrates

Hooded Merganser

Lophodytes cucullatus

Size: Up to 1½ feet long; wingspan of 2 feet; weighs 1–2 pounds

Habitat: Wooded lakes and streams, marshes, small rivers, and woodlands adjacent to bodies of water

Range: They can be found throughout the state of Michigan during the breeding seasons. Several populations can be found across the United States and Canada.

Food: Fish, tadpoles, aquatic insects, and crustaceans

Nesting: May to June

Nest: Nests are shallow, bowl shaped, and made inside tree cavities or human-made wooden duck-nesting structures. Down feathers and wood chips are added to the cavity.

Eggs: 10–12 white eggs

Young: After a month of incubation, eggs will hatch, and ducklings will leave the nest within 24 hours of hatching. They can fly after about 65 days.

Predators: Hawks, humans, snakes, mink, woodpeckers, and martens

Migration: They travel to southern states for the winter.

Hooded Merganser males have a black-and-white crest that distinguishes them from females. Other identifying features include brilliant yellow eyes, black-and-white feathers on its breast and back, and a brown side. The females are duller with a brown crest on the back of the head, brown feathers, and brown eyes.

Did you know?

These are the birds you'll often see flying around in big box stores like Home Depot, Menards, and the like. House Finches are native to the southwestern United States and Mexico. They were once sold in pet stores and were intentionally released by their owners to avoid being caught by the police. Today they can be found in every US state except Alaska and Hawaii.

Nest Type

House Finch

Haemorhous mexicanus

Size: 5–6 inches long; wingspan of 9½ inches; weighs almost an ounce

Habitat: Deserts, grasslands, scrub areas, forests, and suburban and urban areas

Range: House Finches are found statewide in Michigan; they can be found in southern Canada, across the United States, and in most of Mexico.

Food: Insects, seeds, nuts, grains, fruits, and flowers

Nesting: March to August

Nest: Females build the cup-shaped nest in 2 days.

Eggs: 3–6 green or bluish eggs with black spots

Young: Chicks hatch 12–14 days after being laid. Young are blind and naked when they hatch. After about 19 days, they leave the nest.

Predators: Rats, Eastern Chipmunks, American Crows, Blue Jays, raccoons, snakes, and cats

Migration: They are usually permanent residents, but a few birds will migrate southward.

The male House Finch's head and shoulders are red; the hue of the red is based on what berries and fruit they eat. Females and juveniles lack the red color; instead, they are brown with a smudge-like pattern of dark and light brown on the belly.

Did you know?

When viewed straight-on, the yellow portion on the Mallard's bill resembles a cartoon dog's head. All domesticated ducks share the Mallard as their ancestor. Mallard feathers are waterproof; they use oil from the preen gland beneath their feathers to help aid in repelling water. Mallards are the most common duck in the United States and Michigan.

Nest Type   Migrates

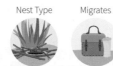

Mallard

Anas platyrhynchos

Size: 24 inches long; wingspan of 36 inches; weighs 2.5–3 pounds

Habitat: Lakes, ponds, rivers, and swamps

Range: They are found throughout Michigan; the population stretches across the United States and Canada into Mexico and as far up as central Alaska.

Food: Insects, worms, snails, aquatic vegetation, sedge seeds, grasses, snails, and wild rice

Nesting: April to May

Nest: The nest is constructed on the ground, near a body of water.

Eggs: 9–13 eggs

Young: Eggs hatch 26–28 days after being laid. The ducklings are fully feathered and have the ability to swim at the time of hatching. Ducklings are cared for until they're 2–3 months old and reach reproductive maturity at 1 year old.

Predators: Humans, crows, mink, coyotes, raccoons, and snapping turtles

Migration: After breeding season, a lot of the population will migrate south; others will stay in familiar areas that have adequate food and shelter.

Male Mallards are gray with an iridescent green head with a tinge of purple spotting, a white line along the collar, rusty-brown chest, yellow bill, and orange legs and feet. Females are dull brown with a purple/blue spot near the rear of the body, a black-and-orange bill, and orange feet.

Did you know?

Cardinals are very territorial and will sometimes attack their own reflection thinking that it is another cardinal that has entered its territory. The early bird gets the worm, and cardinals are some of the first birds active in the morning.

Nest Type

Northern Cardinal

Cardinalis cardinalis

Size: 8–9 inches long; wingspan of 12 inches

Habitat: Hardwood forests, urban areas, orchards, backyards, and fields

Range: They are found in southern and central Michigan, as well as the eastern and midwestern parts of the United States.

Food: Seeds, fruits, insects, spiders, and centipedes

Nesting: March to April

Nest: The cup-shaped nest is built by females in thick foliage, usually at least 1 foot off the ground. It can be 3 inches tall and 4 inches wide.

Eggs: 2–5 off-white colored eggs

Young: 2 weeks after eggs are laid, chicks will hatch with eyes closed and naked besides sparsely placed down feathers.

Predators: Hawks, owls, and squirrels

Migration: Cardinals do not migrate.

Northern Cardinal males are bright-red birds with a black face. Females are a washed-out red or brown in color. Both males and females have a crest (tuft of feathers on the head), and orange beaks and legs. Cardinals can be identified by their laser-gun-like call.

Did you know?

The Osprey is nicknamed the "Fish Hawk" because it is the only hawk in North America that mainly eats live fish. An osprey will rotate its catch to put it in line with its body, pointing head first, which allows for less resistance in flight as the air travels over the fish.

Nest Type   Migrates

Osprey

Pandion haliaetus

Size: 21–23 inches long; wingspan of 59–71 inches; weighs 3–4½ pounds

Habitat: Near lakes, ponds, rivers, swamps, and reservoirs

Range: Most of Michigan during the breeding and migration seasons. Throughout the US and Canada and Alaska

Food: Feeds mostly on fish; they sometimes eat mammals, birds, and reptiles if fish sources are low.

Nesting: For ospreys that migrate, egg-laying happens in April and May. The female will take on most of the incubation of the eggs, as well as the jobs of keeping the offspring warm and providing protection.

Nest: Platform nests are constructed out of twigs and sticks. Nests are constructed on trees, snags, or human-made objects like cellular towers and telephone poles.

Eggs: 1–4 eggs that are cream to brown with a pink hue; eggs have splotches of various shades of brown and pinkish red on them.

Young: Chicks hatch around 36 days after laying and have brown and white down feathers. Osprey fledge around 50–55 days after hatching and will receive care from parents for another 2 months or so.

Predators: Owls, eagles, foxes, skunks, raccoons, snakes

Migration: Ospreys migrate south to wintering areas in the fall.

Ospreys are raptors sporting a brown upper body and white lower body. The wings are brown on the outside and white on the underside with brown spotting and streaks towards the edge. The head is white with a brown band that goes through the eye area, highlighting the yellow eyes.

Did you know?

The Red-tailed Hawk is the most abundant hawk in North America. The Red-tailed Hawk's scream is the sound effect that you hear when soaring eagles are shown in movies. Eagles do not screech like hawks, so filmmakers use hawk calls instead! Red-tailed Hawks can't move their eyes, so they have to move their entire head in order to get a better view around them.

Nest Type   Migrates

Red-tailed Hawk

Buteo jamaicensis

Size: 19–25 inches long; wingspan of 47–57 inches; weighs 2½–4 pounds

Habitat: Forests, deserts, woodlands, grasslands, and farm fields

Range: They are found throughout Michigan and throughout North America.

Food: Rodents, birds, reptiles, amphibians, bats, and insects

Nesting: Hawks mate for life; nesting starts in March.

Nest: Both the male and female help build a large cup-shaped nest, which can be over 6 feet high and 3 feet across; the nest is made of sticks and branches; nests are built at forest edges mostly in the crowns of trees, but hawks will also nest on windowsills and other human-made structures.

Eggs: 1–5 eggs; the insides of eggs are a greenish color.

Young: After 30 days, young (chicks) will hatch. It takes around 10 weeks for the hatchlings to learn to fly and leave the nest.

Predators: Great-horned Owls and crows

Migration: Birds in the northern areas of range will migrate short distances to warmer areas, while the hawks in the southern part of the state do not migrate.

Red-tailed Hawks are named for their rusty-red tails! They have brown heads and a chest that's cream to light brown with brown streaking in the form of a band. Red-tailed Hawks are highly territorial, and throughout the day they will take to the air to look for invaders.

Did you know?
Rose-breasted Grosbeaks are famous for their melodic songs. During the mating season, males may sing up to 689 songs in a day while advertising their breeding territories. Rose-breasted Grosbeaks are very strong fliers; during migration, they are able to fly through the Gulf of Mexico without stopping, which is over 500 miles (805 km)!

Nest Type   Migrates

Rose-breasted Grosbeak

Pheucticus ludovicianus

Size: 7–8½ inches long; wingspan of 11½–13 inches; weighs 1½–2 ounces

Habitat: Forests, forest edges, shrubby areas, swamps, and other wetlands

Range: Can be found throughout Michigan and much of the northeastern United States. During the breeding season, it is a common bird in portions of the Midwest; during migration, it's common in the eastern US.

Food: Omnivores that eat mostly insects and other invertebrates (animals without bones) like spiders and snails. Seeds are also a big portion of their diet.

Nesting: Females lay 1 or 3 broods (groups) of 3–5 eggs a year. Both parents incubate and provide care to young.

Nest: Cup-shaped nest built out of twigs, weeds, and leaves

Eggs: Light greenish or bluish eggs that can be spotted with a brownish red

Young: Chicks are born with just a small number of feathers about 11 days after laying. They will leave the nest 9–12 days after hatching and will be completely independent around the 3-week mark.

Predators: Blue Jays, hawks, grackles, squirrels

Migration: Migrates twice a year in the spring and fall, usually flying during the night hours

Males and females have different appearances, with the male having a white bill, black head, a white belly with a rose-colored throat that extends downs towards parts of the white breast. Females are not as colorful; they have a brown back and off-white-to-cream-colored belly with brown streaks.

Did you know?

The smallest bird that you can find in Michigan is the Ruby-throated Hummingbird. During migration, male hummingbirds will utilize sapsucker (woodpecker) sap wells to get nutrients because of the lack of flowering plants in early spring. Hummingbirds can achieve 200 wing beats per second.

Nest Type

Migrates

Ruby-throated Hummingbird

Archilochus colubris

Size: 3–3½ inches long; wingspan of 3⅛–4¼ inches; weighs ⅒ of an ounce

Habitat: Forested areas, orchards, gardens, and city parks

Range: They can be found throughout the state of Michigan; they breed in the eastern United States and eastern and central Canada.

Food: Drinks nectar from flowers and eats small insects and spiders

Nesting: March to July

Nest: A walnut-size nest is built in dense coverage of trees and shrubs, usually 10–20 feet off the ground; nest can be made of grasses, spider webs, and other vegetation.

Eggs: 2 white eggs

Young: Young (chicks) will start flying around 20 days after hatching.

Predators: Cats, spiders, robber flies, praying mantises, dragonflies, frogs, hawks, and kites (birds of prey)

Migration: Hummingbirds migrate to Mexico or Central America starting in August.

Ruby-throated Hummingbirds are the only species of hummingbirds that nest in the eastern United States. Males have a magnificent ruby-colored throat made of iridescent (shimmering) feathers; males also have green iridescent feathers on their wings. Females are duller in comparison.

Did you know?
The Sandhill Crane is the most abundant crane species in the world. They are not afraid to defend themselves when threatened. They will use their feet and bill to ward off predators, often stabbing attackers with their bill. Sometimes Sandhill Cranes will travel 500 miles in one day to find food.

Nest Type   Migrates

Sandhill Crane

Grus canadensis

Size: 3½–4 feet long; wingspan of 6–7 feet; weighs 7½–10 pounds

Habitat: Grasslands, savannas, and farm fields

Range: Breeding resident that can be found throughout Michigan; found year-round in parts of Florida and Georgia. Can be found during migration in many states along the multiple migration routes like South Carolina, Kansas, Oklahoma, Wyoming, and other states.

Food: Berries, insects, snails, amphibians, and small mammals as well as food crops like corn

Nesting: Nonmigratory populations will lay eggs from December to August, while populations that migrate will nest between April and May.

Nest: Both adults build the cup-shaped nest using vegetation from nearby areas.

Eggs: Up to 3 pale brownish-yellow eggs with brown spots

Young: Chicks are born with the ability to see and walk. Chicks become independent at around 9 months and will start breeding between 2 and 7 years.

Predators: Coyotes, raccoons, ravens, Great Horned Owls, and humans

Migration: Cranes arrive in late March to early May and migrate south from September into December.

The Sandhill Crane is a large bird with gray to brownish feathers with a white face and ruby-red crown. They are commonly seen in large groups in fields.

Did you know?

Snowy Owls are one of the few species of owls that are diurnal, which means they hunt during the daytime, while most of the other owls hunt at night. Snowy Owls can hunt over 1,500 lemmings (small rodents related to voles) in a single year. Because of their thick feathers, Snowy Owls are the largest owls in North America by weight.

Nest Type   Migrates

Snowy Owl

Bubo scandiacus

Size: 20½–28 inches; wingspan of 49½–57 inches; weighs 56½–104 ounces

Habitat: Prairies, fields, marshes, farmland

Range: During the winter, they can be found throughout the state of Michigan; they can also be found throughout New England and westward to Washington State.

Food: Small mammals, especially lemmings (a rodent). They also eat birds.

Nesting: Snowy Owls usually breed during the months of May and September. Males court females using a mix of displays, one performed while in the air and the other performed while on the ground.

Nest: Females build the nest by hollowing out an area on the ground and using her body to make the nest shape.

Eggs: Usually 3–11 white eggs, about 2 inches long and wide, are laid per brood.

Young: Chicks or owlets hatch blind with downy feathers 30 days after laying. Chicks receive care from both parents. After about 14–25 days, chicks will venture out from the nest.

Predators: Foxes, wolves, dogs, humans

Migration: They migrate south from extreme northern Canada and Alaska to interior and southern Canada and the northern US during the winter.

Snowy Owls are white with brown bars and spots. The males are a more brilliant and vibrant white, while the females are darker in color with more spots and bars than the males. Both males and females have bright-yellow eyes.

Did you know?

White-breasted Nuthatches are all about home security. When leaving the nesting cavity, White-breasted Nuthatches will put pieces of fur or vegetation around their home to make it harder for predators to smell the nest. Sometimes they will take it a step further and rub Blister Beetles near the entrance; the smell from the Blister Beetles will deter squirrels from invading the nest.

Nest Type

White-breasted Nuthatch

Sitta carolinensis

Size: 6 inches long; wingspan of 11 inches; weighs ½–1 ounce

Habitat: Mature forests, parks, woodland edges, and suburban areas

Range: They can be found throughout Michigan; their range extends from the East Coast of the US to the West Coast and as far up as central Canada.

Food: Insects, grubs, seeds, ants, spiders, and berries

Nesting: May to June

Nest: Females will build nests in natural cavities or old woodpecker cavities. Sometimes they will enlarge the cavities.

Eggs: 5–8 eggs that come in a variety of colors from creamy white to a light pink or red hue, sometimes speckled

Young: Chicks hatch after 14 days and are born naked and blind. Both parents feed the young; they leave the nest 14–24 days after hatching.

Predators: Snakes, woodpeckers, squirrels, and hawks

Migration: They are a permanent resident (do not migrate).

A White-breasted Nuthatch is a small bird with gray on its back; a white face and belly area; and black eyes, bill, and strip on the top of its head. People often mistake a White-breasted Nuthatch for a woodpecker because of the similar ways it nests in tree cavities and climbs trees. Nuthatches will hide food in a variety of places like under bark, in snow, and under moss and other vegetation.

Did you know?

A turkey can fly at night and will land in trees to roost. Turkeys have some interesting facial features; the red skin growth on a turkey's face above the beak is called a snood, while the growth under the beak is called a wattle. Wild Turkeys can have more than 5,000 feathers.

Nest Type

Wild Turkey

Meleagris gallopavo

Size: 3–4 feet long; wingspan of 5 feet; males weigh 16–25 pounds; females weigh 9–11 pounds

Habitat: Woodlands and grasslands

Range: Common in the Lower Peninsula and southern parts of the Upper Peninsula. They also can be found in the eastern US and have been introduced in many western areas of the country.

Food: Grain, snakes, frogs, insects, acorns, berries, and ferns

Nesting: April to June

Nest: The nest is built on the ground using leaves as bedding, in brush or near the base of trees.

Eggs: 10–12 tan eggs with reddish-brown spots

Young: Poults (young) hatch about a month after eggs are laid; they will flock with the mother for a year. When young are unable to fly, the mom will stay on the ground with her poults to provide protection and warmth. When poults grow up, they are considered a hen if they are female, or a gobbler or tom if they are male.

Predators: Humans, foxes, raccoons, owls, eagles, skunks, and fishers (birds of prey)

Migration: Turkeys do not migrate.

A Wild Turkey is a large bird that is dark brown and black with some iridescent feathers. Males will fan out their tail to attract a mate. When threatened, they will also fan out their tail and rush the predator, sometimes kicking and puncturing prey with the spurs on their feet.

Did you know?

Wood Ducks will "mimic" a soccer player when a predator is near their young: they flop! Female Wood Ducks will fake a broken wing to lure predators away from her young. Wood Duck hatchlings must jump from the nest after hatching to reach the water. They can jump 50 feet or more without hurting themselves.

Nest Type

Migrates

Wood Duck

Aix sponsa

Size: 15–20 inches long; wingspan of 30 inches; weighs about a pound

Habitat: Swamps, woody ponds, and marshes

Range: They are found throughout Michigan; during the breeding season they're found in the northern parts of the state. Wood Ducks are year-long residents in central and southern Michigan; they are also in the eastern US, southern Mexico, the Pacific Northwest, and on the West Coast.

Food: Fruits, nuts, and aquatic vegetation, especially duckweed, sedges, and grasses

Nesting: March to June

Nest: Wood Ducks use hollow trees, abandoned woodpecker cavities, and human-made nesting boxes.

Eggs: 8–15 white eggs are laid once a year. Sometimes females will lay eggs in another female's nest; this process is called egg dumping.

Young: Eggs hatch about a month after being laid. Chicks will leave the nest after a day and fly within 8 weeks.

Predators: Raccoons, mink, fish, hawks, Snapping Turtles, owls, humans, and muskrats

Migration: They migrate south in winter and north in spring using the Mississippi flyway

Wood Duck males have a brightly colored crest (tuft of feathers) of iridescent (shimmering) green, red, and purple, with a mahogany brown upper breast area and tan bottom. Males also have red eyes. Females are brown to gray. Wood Ducks have strong claws that enable them to climb up trees into cavities.

Did you know?

The American Toad is the mostly commonly observed toad in Michigan. While the American Toad has warts on it, you cannot get warts from touching it. Toads are toxic (but not to humans); they have two parotid glands, one behind each eye that produces a toxin they release to prevent predators from eating them.

Most Active

American Toad

Anaxyrus americanus

Size: 2–4 inches long; weighs 1½–2 ounces

Habitat: Prairies, forests, suburban areas, swamps, and other wetlands

Range: They are found throughout Michigan and from New England south into parts of Mississippi, Alabama, and Georgia.

Food: Insects, algae, worms, snails, ants, moths, and beetles

Mating: February to July

Nest: No nest

Eggs: 2,000–19,000 or more eggs are laid in bodies of water attached to vegetation or the bottom of shallow water.

Young: Eggs hatch 3–10 days after laying. They will stay in the tadpole stage 40–65 days. It takes 2–3 years to reach reproductive maturity.

Predators: Hognoses and other snakes, raccoons, and birds; as tadpoles: beetles, crayfish, birds, and dragonfly larvae

The American Toad has a brown-to-clay-red-colored base layer with brown and black spots and noticeable warts on its body. During the summer or extreme heat, toads can reduce their metabolic rate and cool themselves down.

Did you know?

Garter Snakes are highly social and will form groups with other snakes and often other species to overwinter together in a burrow or hole. When threatened by a predator or handled, they will sometimes musk or emit a foul-smelling, oily substance from their cloaca (butt).

Most Active

Eastern Garter Snake

Thamnophis sirtalis

Size: 14–36 inches long (rarely over 17 inches); weighs 5–5½ ounces

Habitat: Forests and forest edges, grasslands, and suburban areas

Range: They are found throughout Michigan and can be found in the eastern US from Minnesota, southward to eastern Texas, and then east towards the Atlantic coast.

Food: Frogs, snails, toads, salamanders, insects, fish, and worms

Mating: April or May

Nest: No nest; they will use natural cavities in the ground or abandoned burrows of small mammals.

Eggs: No eggs are laid. Garter Snakes are born live in a litter of between 8 and 20 snakes.

Young: Snakelets are 4½–9 inches long at birth; no parental care is given.

Predators: Crows, ravens, hawks, owls, raccoons, foxes, and squirrels

Eastern Garter Snakes are black with three yellow stripes running down their body on the back and sides. They withstand winter by gathering in groups inside the burrows of rodents or under human-made structures, and they enter brumation, or a state of slowed body activity.

Did you know?

The Eastern Massasauga Rattlesnake is the only venomous snake that calls Michigan home! It is also known as the "Swamp Rattler" because it is often found in or close to swamp areas. Eastern Massasaugas rarely strike humans; instead, they prefer to stay still and hide, sometimes not even rattling they could be discovered. **Safety Note:** These snakes are venomous (toxic). If you see one, observe or admire from a distance.

Most Active

Eastern Massasauga Rattlesnake

Sistrurus catenatus

Size: 23–30 inches long; weighs 10½–14 ounces

Habitat: Swamps, marshes, bogs, wetlands, as well as meadows, wet prairies, and grasslands

Range: Massasaugas can be found throughout the states that touch the Great Lakes, as well as portions of Canada, Iowa, and Missouri. In Michigan, they can be found throughout the state, including a small area in the Upper Peninsula.

Food: Small snakes, small mammals such as rodents, lizards, and invertebrates like centipedes

Mating: Massasaugas breeding season happens in the spring but can also occur in the fall.

Nest: Abandoned mammal dens or downed logs

Eggs: Does not produce eggs; gives live birth to young

Young: 3–3½ months after mating, 5–20 snakelets are born via live birth in abandoned burrows or downed logs. Young are fully developed when born and will only stay a few days with mom before venturing out on their own. They become mature around 3 or 4 years old.

Predators: Humans, raptors, wild cats

Eastern Massasaugas come in a variety of colors from gray and light brown to deep brown and black with dark-colored patches with a light outline around them. They have thick bodies with an arrow- or triangle-shaped head. They have cat-like eyes or vertical pupils. At the base of the tail is a rattle the snake uses to alert would-be threats of its presence.

Did you know?

Eastern Newts have a toxin that they release through their skin that makes potential predators sick. The bright-orange color of an Eastern Newt acts as a warning system to would-be predators that they taste bad or are toxic.

Most Active

Eastern Newt

Notophthalmus viridescens

Size: 3–5 inches long; weighs less than a dime

Habitat: Near and in streams, marshes, lakes, and ponds; in woodlands or woody areas

Range: Throughout much of Michigan; found from New England and the Atlantic Coast and west as far as Texas

Food: Aquatic insects, snails, worms, amphibians, and fish eggs.

Mating: Breeding season for the Eastern Newt starts in the winter and finishes in early spring.

Nest: No true nest; eggs are laid underwater.

Eggs: Females lay eggs in the spring, in still or quiet water. Eggs attach to underwater vegetation. Females lay 200—400 eggs, providing no form of care.

Young: The Eastern Newt larvae hatches around 3–8 weeks after an egg is laid. Larvae transform into an eft (juvenile) by the end of summer. Efts live on land for 1—3 years. When mature, they return to the water for the remainder of their lives.

Predators: Fish, birds, insects, amphibians, and reptiles

The Eastern Newt goes through three life stages. It has a fully aquatic or water-living stage as a larva. During this stage, it has gills and a flat tail. In the next stage (the juvenile stage), they live on land. This stage of life is called the red eft stage. During this stage, they sport rough, bright-red skin with red spots and have a rounded tail. The last stage is the adult stage, where they have a brownish-yellow to olive-brown color on the upper half of the body with red spots outlined by black circles, and a yellow underside with black spots on it.

Did you know?

The Eastern Tiger Salamander can grow up to 13 inches long and live over 20 years! Eastern Tiger Salamanders migrate to their birthplace in order to breed, sometimes over a mile or more. Eastern Tiger Salamanders have a hidden weapon! They produce a poisonous toxin that is secreted or released from two glands in their tail. This toxin makes them taste bad to predators and allows them to escape.

Most Active

Eastern Tiger Salamander

Ambystoma tigrinum

Size: 7–13 inches long; weighs 4½ ounces

Habitat: Woodlands, marshes, and meadows; they spend most of their time underground in burrows.

Range: In Michigan, they can be found throughout the state except for northeastern areas bordering the Great Lakes and the Upper Peninsula. Populations are also found in the western United States.

Food: Carnivores (eat meat); insects, frogs, worms, and snails

Mating: Tiger Salamanders leave their burrows to find standing bodies of fresh water. They breed in late winter and early spring after the ground has thawed.

Nest: No nest, but eggs are joined together into one group in a jelly-like sack called an egg mass. An egg mass is attached to grass, leaves, and other plant material at the bottom of a pond.

Eggs: There are 20–100 eggs or more in an egg mass.

Young: Eggs hatch after 2 weeks and the young are fully aquatic with external gills. Limbs develop shortly after hatching; within 3 months, the young are fully grown but will hang around in a vernal pool. Individuals living in permanent ponds can take up to 6 months to fully develop.

Predators: Adults: Snakes, owls, and badgers; Young: diving beetles, fish, turtles, and herons

Eastern Tiger Salamanders have thick black, brown, or grayish bodies with uneven spots of yellow, tan, brown, or green along the head and body. The underside is usually a variation of yellow. Males are usually larger and thicker than females.

129

Did you know?

The Eastern Hognose Snake is venomous! But its venom is not harmful to us. The Hognose's teeth have a dual purpose: they inject venom into prey and also deflate toads who puff their bodies up to avoid being eaten. The Hognose wards off would-be predators by flattening its head to look like a cobra. If that doesn't work, it will play dead by flipping its body over and letting its tongue hang out of its mouth.

Most Active

Hognose Snake

Heterodon platirhinos

Size: 2–2½ feet long; weighs 2–4 ounces

Habitat: Shrublands, prairies, grasslands, coastal areas, and forests

Range: In Michigan, they can be found throughout the Lower Peninsula of the state and a small area of the southern part of the Upper Peninsula, to an expansive range southward into Florida and westward into Texas and parts of Kansas.

Food: Frogs, toads, salamanders, birds, and invertebrates

Mating: April and May

Nest: Hognose Snakes dig burrows and will lay eggs under rocks, leaves, or in rotting logs.

Eggs: In June to July they will dig a burrow and lay 8–40 eggs (average clutch is around 25).

Young: 60 days after being laid, the eggs hatch. They do not receive care from parents at birth. Snakes reach full maturity around 20 months.

Predators: Hawks, snakes, raccoons, and opossums

The Hognose is a thick-bodied snake that gets its name from its shovel-like snout that it uses to dig in soil. They come in a variety of colors from red and brown to gray and black; they even come in versions of orange and red. Their underbody is lighter than their top.

Did you know?

Leopards are used by humans in many ways, including research for medical projects, as well as serving as specimens for biology courses. During the winter, they will hibernate underwater in ponds that have lots of oxygen and do not freeze.

Most Active

Northern Leopard Frog

Lithobates pipiens

Size: 2½–4½ inches long; weighs ½–3 ounces

Habitat: Meadows, open fields, lakes, forest edges, and ponds

Range: They are found throughout Michigan; there are strong populations into Canada and throughout the northeastern states to Iowa, with populations extending into northern California, the Pacific Northwest, and the Southwest.

Food: Spiders, worms, insects, and other invertebrates like crustaceans and mollusks

Mating: Late March to early June; mating occurs in water.

Nest: No nest is constructed; within 3 days of mating, the female will lay eggs in permanent shallow bodies of water attached to vegetation just below the surface.

Eggs: A few hundred to 7,000 or more eggs are laid in one egg mass that is 2–5 inches wide.

Young: Tadpoles hatch after about 2–3 weeks of being laid and then complete the metamorphic cycle to become frogs in around 3 months. They reach reproductive maturity in the first or second year for males and within 2–3 years for females.

Predators: Fish, frogs, herons, snakes, hawks, gulls, mink, turtles, and dragonfly larvae

The Northern Leopard Frog is a smooth-skinned frog with 2–3 rows of dark spots with a lighter outline around them, atop a brown or green base layer. It has a ridge that extends from the base of the eye to the rear of the frog's bum. They have a white underside. Juveniles (young) will use streams and drainage ditches with vegetation to reach seasonal habitats.

Did you know?

The Snapping Turtle is the largest turtle that can be found in Michigan. The Snapping Turtle's sex is determined by the temperature of the nest! Nest temperatures that are 67–68 degrees produce females, temperatures in the range between 70 and 72 degrees produce both males and females, and nests that are 73–75 degrees will usually produce all males.

Most Active

Snapping Turtle

Chelydra serpentina

Size: 8–16 inches long; weighs 10–35 pounds

Habitat: Rivers, marshes, and lakes; can be found in areas that have brackish water (freshwater and saltwater mixture)

Range: They are found throughout Michigan; also found in the eastern US and southern Canada.

Food: These omnivores (eat both plants and animals) eat frogs, reptiles, snakes, birds, small mammals, and plants.

Mating: April to November are the breeding months; lays eggs during June and July

Nest: Females dig a hole in sandy soil and lay the eggs into them.

Eggs: 25–42 eggs, sometimes as many as 80 or more

Young: Like Sea Turtles, Snapping Turtles have temperature dependent sex determination (TSD), meaning the temperature of the nest determines the sex of the young. Hatchlings leave the nest between August and October. In the North, turtles mature around 15 to 20 years, while southern turtles mature around 12 years old.

Predators: Raccoons, skunks, crows, dogs, and humans

Snapping Turtle's carapace (top shell) is dark green to brown and usually covered in algae or moss. The plastron or bottom of the shell is smaller than the carapace. They are crepuscular animals that are mostly active during the dawn and dusk hours. Young turtles will actively look for food. As adults, they rely heavily on ambushing to hunt; they bury themselves in the sand with just the tip of their nose and eyes showing.

Did you know?

Spring Peepers get their name because their chirp call usually coordinates with the beginning of spring. They are able to prevent their blood from freezing during the winter due to an adaptation in their blood that acts like antifreeze. Spring Peepers' calls or chirps can be heard over a mile away!

Most Active

Spring Peeper

Pseudacris crucifer

Size: About 1–1½ inches long; weighs about as much as a penny

Habitat: Woodlands, forest edges, suburban areas, ponds, swamps, and other wetlands

Range: Widespread throughout the state of Michigan; their range extends throughout northeastern Canada downward to north Florida and eastward into east Texas.

Food: Insects

Mating: Their mating takes place between March and June, in or near ponds and other bodies of still water.

Nest: No nest building occurs. Eggs are laid and then attach to underwater vegetation and debris at the bottom of shallow ponds.

Eggs: They typically lay 800–1,000 eggs; each egg is covered in a jelly-like coat.

Young: 3–4 days after egg laying, eggs will hatch into tadpoles. Over the next 7–8 weeks, tadpoles will go through a transformation called metamorphosis and turn into frogs.

Predators: Birds, fish, rats, snakes, wading birds like herons, otters, and raptors

The Spring Peeper is brown to tan in color with a dark X on its back. Males are smaller than the females and usually have a darker throat. Spring peepers are more active during the night, where the darkness provides extra protection from the fewer predators that are out during the night.

Glossary

Adaptation—An animal's physical (outward) or behavioral (inward) adjustment to changes in the environment.

Amphibian—A small animal with a backbone, has moist skin, and lacks scales. Most amphibians start out as an egg, live at least part of their life in water, and finish life as a land dweller.

Biome—A part or region of Earth that has a particular type of climate and animals and plants that adapted to live in the area.

Bird—A group of animals that all have two eyes, two legs and feet, a beak, feathers, and wings; while not all birds fly, all birds lay eggs.

Brood—A group of young birds that hatch at the same time and with the same mother.

Carnivore—An animal that primarily eats other animals.

Clutch—The number of eggs a bird lays during one nesting period; birds can lay more than one clutch each season.

Crepuscular—The hours before sunset or just after sunrise; some animals have adapted to be most active during these low-light times.

Diurnal—During the day; many animals are most active during the daytime.

Ecosystem—A group of animals and plants that interact with each other and the physical area that they live in.

Evolution—A process of change in a species or a group of animals that are all the same kind; evolution happens over several generations or in a group of animals living around the same time; evolution happens through adaptation, or physical and biological changes to better fit the environment over time.

Fledgling—A baby bird that has developed flight feathers and has left the nest.

Gestation—The length of time a bird is carried in its mother's womb.

Herbivore—An animal that primarily eats plants and other vegetation.

Hibernate—A survival strategy or process where animals "slow down" and go into a long period of reduced activity to survive winter or seasonal changes; during hibernation, activities like feeding, breathing, and converting food to energy all can slow down.

Incubate—When a bird warms eggs by sitting on them.

Invasive—A nonnative animal that outcompetes native animals in a particular area, harming the environment.

Mammal—An air-breathing, warm-blooded, fur- or hair-covered animal with a backbone. All mammals produce milk and usually give birth to live young.

Migration—When animals move from one area to another. Migration usually occurs seasonally, but it can also happen due to biological processes, such as breeding.

Molt—When animals shed or drop their skin, feathers, or shell.

Nocturnal—At night; many animals are most active at night.

Nonnative—An organism introduced (usually by humans) into a new area.

Omnivore—An animal that eats both plants and other animals.

Predator—An animal that hunts (and eats) other animals.

Raptor—A group of birds that all have a curved beak and sharp talons, which hunt or feed on other animals. Also known as a bird of prey.

Reptile—An egg-laying, air-breathing, cold-blooded animal that has a backbone and skin made of scales, which crawls on its stomach or uses stubby legs to get around.

Scat—The waste product that animals release from their bodies; another word for it is poop or droppings.

Talon—The claw on the feet of a raptor or bird of prey.

Torpor—A form of hibernation in which an animal slows down its breathing, feeding, and heart rate; torpor ranges from a few hours at a time to a whole day; torpor does not involve a deep sleep.

Checklist

Mammals

- [ ] American Badger
- [ ] American Beaver
- [ ] Black Bear
- [ ] Bobcat
- [ ] Coyote
- [ ] Eastern Chipmunk
- [ ] Eastern Cottontail
- [ ] Eastern Fox Squirrel
- [ ] Elk
- [ ] Gray Wolf
- [ ] Little Brown Bat
- [ ] Long-tailed Weasel
- [ ] Meadow Vole
- [ ] Mink
- [ ] Moose
- [ ] North American Porcupine
- [ ] Northern Raccoon
- [ ] Northern River Otter
- [ ] Red Fox
- [ ] Snowshoe Hare
- [ ] Southern Flying Squirrel
- [ ] Virginia Opossum
- [ ] White-tailed Deer
- [ ] Wolverine
- [ ] Woodchuck (Groundhog)

Birds

- [ ] American Goldfinch
- [ ] American Redstart
- [ ] American Robin
- [ ] Bald Eagle
- [ ] Barred Owl
- [ ] Belted Kingfisher
- [ ] Black-capped Chickadee
- [ ] Blue Jay
- [ ] Canada Goose
- [ ] Common Loon
- [ ] Eastern Bluebird
- [ ] Eastern Meadowlark/ Western Meadowlark
- [ ] Great Blue Heron
- [ ] Great Horned Owl
- [ ] Green-winged Teal
- [ ] Hairy/Downy Woodpecker
- [ ] Hooded Merganser
- [ ] House Finch

- [ ] Mallard
- [ ] Northern Cardinal
- [ ] Osprey
- [ ] Red-tailed Hawk
- [ ] Rose-breasted Grosbeak
- [ ] Ruby-throated Hummingbird
- [ ] Sandhill Crane
- [ ] Snowy Owl
- [ ] White-breasted Nuthatch
- [ ] Wild Turkey
- [ ] Wood Duck

Reptiles and Amphibians

- [ ] American Toad
- [ ] Eastern Garter Snake
- [ ] Eastern Massasauga Rattlesnake
- [ ] Eastern Newt
- [ ] Eastern Tiger Salamander
- [ ] Hognose Snake
- [ ] Northern Leopard Frog
- [ ] Snapping Turtle
- [ ] Spring Peeper

The Art of Conservation®

Featuring two signature programs, The Songbird Art Contest™ and Fish Art Contest®, the Art of Conservation programs celebrate the arts as a cornerstone to conservation. To enter, youth artists create an original hand-drawn illustration and written essay, story, or poem synthesizing what they have learned. The contests are FREE and open to students in K-12. For program updates, rules, guidelines, and entry forms, visit: www.TheArtofConservation.org

The Fish Art Contest® introduces youth to the wonders of fish, the joy of fishing, and the importance of aquatic conservation. The Fish Art Contest uses art, science, and creative writing to foster connections to the outdoors and inspire the next generation of stewards. Participants are encouraged to use the Fish On! lesson plan, then submit an original, handmade piece of artwork to compete for prizes and international recognition.

The Songbird Art Contest® explores the wonders and species diversity of North American songbirds. Raising awareness and educating the public on bird conservation, the Songbird program builds stewardship, encourages outdoors participation, and promotes the discovery of nature as close as anyone's backyard.

Photo Credits

Dan Lynch: 8 (Chlorastrolite); **Stewart Ragan:** 144
Silhouettes and tracks by Anthony Hertzel unless otherwise noted.
s=silhouette, t=animal track(s)

All images used under license from Shutterstock.com:
ace03: footer burst; **Robert Adami:** 98; **Tristan Adler:** 40; **Agami Photo Agency:** 64; **Airin.dizain:** 44s; **Muhammad Alfatih 05:** 18s; **Jody Ann:** 14; **Lukasz Antoniszyn:** 39; **Victor Arita:** 19; **Joseph M. Arseneau:** 22; **Agnieszka Bacal:** 37, 52; **Raul Baena:** 63; **Bonnie Taylor Barry:** 100; **basel101658:** 38s; **Ghost Bear:** 35; **Michael Benard:** 127, 137; **Gabbie Berry:** 126; **BGSmith:** 16; **Karel Bock:** 133; **Todd Boland:** 117; **Miles Boyer:** 120; **Mark Byer:** 41; **Steve Byland:** 75, 83; **Alpha C:** 26s, 30s, 42s, 58s; **Mark Castiglia:** 17; **Ondrej Chvatal:** 8 (Wolverine); **Romuald Cisakowski:** 34; **Mircea Costina:** 56, 123; **Brooke Crigger:** 8 (Mastadon); **Sandi Cullifer:** 110; **Jim Cumming:** 30; **Gerald A. DeBoer:** 55; **Danita Delimont:** 26, 107; **DarAnna:** 99; **DenisaPro:** 59; **DnDavis:** 89; **Rusty Dodson:** 54; **Fiona M. Donnelly:** 108; **Dennis W Donohue:** 84; **dramaj:** 32s; **Ian Duffield:** 104; **J.A. Dunbar:** 111; **Kozyreva Elena:** 34s, 60s; **Lisa Basile Ellwood:** 60; **Eroshka:** 54s; **Deborah Ferrin:** 21; **Frank Fichtmueller:** 13; **FloridaStock:** 68; **Jiri Foltyn:** 23; **FotoRequest:** 62, 70, 93; **Lev Frid:** 36; **Gallinago_media:** 48s; **Greens and Blues:** 112; **Amanda Guercio:** 130; **Miroslav Halama:** 61; **Kerry Hargrove:** 85; **Elliotte Rusty Harold:** 46; **Harry Collins Photography:** 73, 118; **Ayman Haykal:** 67; **Ray Hennessy:** 81; **Chris Hill:** 88; **Susan Hodgson:** 8 (Monarch); **Karen Hogan:** 92; **Intothewild:** 38; **Malachi Ives:** 71; **Matt Jeppson:** 129; **Vladislav T. Jirousek:** 124; **Joseph Scott Photography:** 87; **Paul Jones Jr:** 78; **Tory Kallman:** 18, 116; **David Kalosson:** 48; **Viktoria Karpunina:** 50s; **Cathy Keifer:** 76, 96; **Keneva Photography:** 94; **Janet M Kessler:** 66; **Krumpelman Photography:** 95; **Geoffrey Kuchera:** 32; **Holly Kuchera:** 31; **Brian F. Kushner:** 53; **Brian Lasenby:** 72, 80, 134; **Dennis Laughlin:** 12; **Bruce MacQueen:** 77; **Karl R. Martin:** 86; **Kazakova Maryia:** 11 (ground nest); **mamita:** 20s; **Don Mammoser:** 105; **Oleg Mayorov:** 91; **David McMillan:** 8 (American Robin); **Martin Mecnarowski:** 103; **Alyssa Metro:** 132; **Jesus_Miguel:** 102; **Millenius:** 8 (WI state flag); **Elly Miller:** 69; **Miloje:** background/inset burst; **MurzillA:** 40s; **ND700:** 114; **Jim Nelson:** 115; **nialat:** 47; **Nina B Nichols:** 8 (Petoskey Stone); **Jay Ondreicka:** 8 (Painted Turtle), 128, 131; **Paul Reeves Photography:** 44, 65, 121; **Pavel K:** 12t; **PC-L-N:** 45; **PCpredragilievski:** 28s; **Rita Petcu:** 43; **pichayasri:** 11 (platform nest), 11 (suitcase); **Rachel Portwood:** 24; **Ondrej Prosicky:** 58; **Rabbitti:** 25, 82; **Tom Reichner:** 42, 51; **rhfletcher:** 90; **Leena Robinson:** 27; **Ron Rowan Photography:** 106; **Jason Patrick Ross:** 122, 136; **RRichard29:** 50; **RT Images:** 113; **Ryguyrguy74:** 15; **Menno Schaefer:** 49; **Ken Schulze:** 8 (White Pine); **Shoriful_is:** 101; **Benjamin Simeneta:** 135; **slowmotiongli:** 8 (Brook Trout); **SofiaV:** 11 (cavity nest); **sreewing:** 28t; **Rostislav Stach:** 28, 29; **stopkin:** 16s; **Dominate Studio:** 12s; **Marek R. Swadzba:** 79; **T_Dub0v:** 11 (cup nest); **Mary Terriberry:** 8 (Apple Blossom); **Paul Tessier:** 57; **Thomas Torget:** 20; **Net Vector:** 58t; **Viktorya170377:** 22s; **Liz Weber:** 33; **w e s o m e 24:** 24s; **Mike Wilhelm:** 125; **Wirestock Creators:** 97; **Brian A Wolf:** 109; **ya_mayka:** 46s; **yvontrep:** 74; **Oral Zirek:** 119

About the Author

Alex Troutman is a wildlife biologist, birder, nature enthusiast, and science communicator from Austell, Georgia. He has a passion for sharing the wonders of nature and introducing the younger generation to the outdoors. He holds both a bachelor's degree and a master's degree in biology from Georgia Southern University (the Real GSU), with a focus in conservation. Because he knows what it feels like to not see individuals who look like you, or come from a similar background, doing 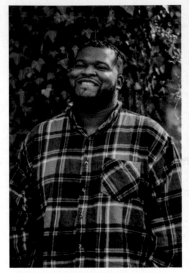 the things you enjoy or working in the career that you aspire to be in, Alex makes a point not only to be that representation for the younger generation, but also to make sure that kids have exposure to the careers they are interested in and the diverse scientists working in those careers.

Alex is the co-organizer of several Black in X weeks, including Black Birders Week, Black Mammologists Week, and Black in Marine Science Week. This movement encourages diversity in nature, the celebration of Black individual scientists, awareness of Black nature enthusiasts, and diversity in STEAM fields.